The 1776 Quilt

Heartache, Heritage, and Happiness

PAM HOLLAND

Breckling Press

Library of Congress Cataloging-in-Publication Data

Holland, Pam.

The 1776 quilt : Heartache, Heritage, and Happiness / Pam Holland.

p. cm.

Includes bibliographical references and index.

ISBN 1-933308-10-9 (pbk.)

1. Quilting--Patterns. 2. Appliqué--Patterns. I. Title.

TT835.H554 2006

746.46092--dc22

2006026396

Editorial direction by Anne Knudsen

Editing and technical editing by Mary Elizabeth Johnson

Cover design by Kim Bartko, produced by Maria Mann

Interior design by Maria Mann

Cover photograph, photographs on pages 102-103, and detail photographs of Pam Holland's *1776* by Sharon Hoogstraten

Interior photographs of new quilts, except pages 102-103, by Philip Martin

Family photographs and all travel photographs by Pam Holland, except page 4 (top left), page 5 (top right), and page 22 (bottom right)

Technical drawings by Eliza Wheeler

This book was set in Centaur, Goudy Sans & Goudy Text

Published by Breckling Press

283 N. Michigan St., Elmhurst, Il 60126

Printed and bound in China

International Standard Book Number: 1-933308-10-9

Dedication

$\mathfrak{I}$ dedicate this book to those of my family who have left us, but whose spirits will remain forever: my daughter, Liseby, whose life was claimed by cancer when she was only 24 years old; Karen, my son's partner, who was killed in an automobile accident; and my son Darrin, who also died in an automobile accident. We love and remember you always.

Liseby

Contents

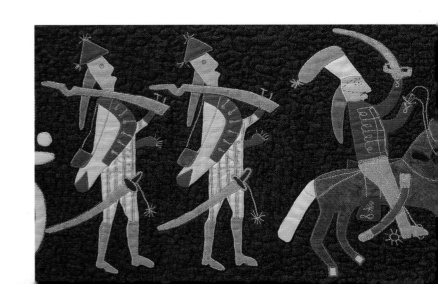

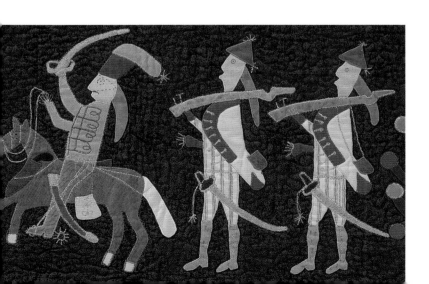

Flickenteppich 1776/1779, Southeast Germany. Inlaid work, pieces of woolen cloth, silk velvet, cotton velvet. Embroidered silk and linen. Presently located in the Stadtmuseum Bautzen, Germany. Regionalmuseum der sächsischen Oberlausitz. Sammlung Oscar Roesger, 1868-1910. Inv.-Nr.: R 5818. Photography by Jürgen Matschie, Bautzen.

1776, appliqué quilt by Pam Holland, 2003.

Preface

I discovered the joys of being creative after a winding and at times painful path through life. My personal journey began when my family moved from the pristine beauty of Launceston, Tasmania, to the bare, brown satellite town of Elizabeth in South Australia. I was often lost in my own world, where I was usually making drawings. My most treasured gift one Christmas was a set of 72 Lakeland color pencils, given by my parents. Mother made a red denim cover to protect the box, and I used those pencils until they were worn to small stubs.

I guess by today's standards we were poor, but, with the innocence of children, we accepted the way we lived and knew no difference. In winter, we huddled around the grey electric three-bar heater, and I slept with Dad's ancient wool dressing gown over me as a blanket. In summer, Elizabeth was desolate, hot, and glaringly bright. The winds from the north whipped across the brown fields that had been cleared to build the city. I remember the huge dust storms that would roll across our school: the color of rust, they were choking and completely frightening to me and my ten-year-old playmates. Many times my brother, sister, and I rushed home through storms like these, seeking the safety and comfort of our kitchen.

The kitchen was the focal point of our daily lives. The radio on the bench was our entertainment. I loved the scripted plays, among them *When a Girl Marries* and *Portia Faces Life.* The silken voice of the announcer crooned, "For those who have loved and those who can remember," transporting me into an imaginary world beyond the realities of school, church on Sundays, and our sparse backyard.

The kitchen was also the place where my mother sewed, her machine propped on the edge of the kitchen table. Even with early and constant exposure to sewing, I had no inclination to become a seamstress. Sewing seemed tedious and, with a mother who was so proficient, there seemed little need for me to learn.

Although I wasn't made to sit at the machine, I did have a role in the sewing process. My job was to draft patterns from my mother's favorite Enid Gilchrist book. First, and at my mother's direction, I rounded up old newspapers from the neighbors. Then, armed with an old ruler and pencil, I spent many hours preparing basic patterns. Will I ever forget those bloomers and shapeless petticoats? It was nearly impossible to see the pencil line through the newsprint, but that's all we had. I can't quite work out why I didn't refuse to do this exacting, and, to me, pointless, task. In retrospect, that saturation of experience would become my grounding in working with fabric, giving me the confidence that led me to become a clothing designer and manufacturer.

Skipping forward to 1984, my life was an interesting mix of mother, fashion designer, shop owner, and manufacturer. Looking back now, I wonder how I ever managed to do all those things and keep my sanity. Keith Holland and I had married in 1967. Seventeen years

ABOVE RIGHT: At ten years of age, here I am (far left), with my brother Robert (now an international ship captain) and sister Jennifer, who grew up to be a radiologist and lives in Malaysia.
BELOW: The windswept landscape of South Australia provided little inspiration to a budding young artist with 72 colored pencils.

later, we had eleven children, eight of them at home. Our three biological children were Jamie, 13, Rachael, 12, and Matthew, 11. Our 16-year-old daughter Suchada ("Susie") had come to us from Thailand five years before with an eye condition that had effectively rendered her blind until she received treatment (in the form of seven different surgeries). We had two sons of Aboriginal descent, Darrin, 13, and Michael, 12, two brothers who had been abandoned by their Mum. (Darrin died in 1997 after suffering an accident two years earlier.) Joshua, our son from Thailand was 7; we adopt-

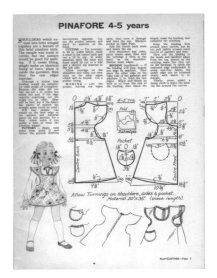

I learned pattern drafting early on, from books like these by Enid Gilchrist.

ed him when he was three weeks old, weighed three pounds, and, as a result of his low body weight, was suffering deafness and epilepsy. Our Sri-Lankan daughter, Callie, whom I had found in an orphanage when she was six months old and weighed six pounds, was four years old now and gaining weight with enthusiasm. A grown son, Phat (known as Danny), was living with his birth parents, whom we had helped move to Australia from Vietnam. Our son Sam had succumbed to congenital birth conditions before he was six. We were also foster parents (to 148 children from 1967 to 2005!), so there were always extra children in the house, who just needed a safe place for a while.

Our house was noisy, happy, and a fun place to live. The washing, ironing, shopping, and cooking were like military maneuvers. Everything ran pretty much like clockwork, to the extent that Matthew thought I did such a good job washing his football uniforms, he brought home those of the entire team at the end of each week. "My Mum will do it," he declared with pride, bless him!

At the same time, I was designing about 100 garments each season for the business, "Mixed Blessings," (the name was a play on the composition of my family) that I owned with my partner Cynthia McLeod. The pressure of business was ever-present, as we designed, manufactured, photographed, and packaged our line of garments. We were quite successful in exporting our garments to Japan as well as selling to the most exclusive shops in Australia, but it was very hard work. And, although I constantly handled fabric, I had no interest in sewing as a hobby, nor in quilting.

Liseby

Because Keith and I had seven adopted from various parts of southeast Asia, I had many friends in the adoption and support communities. During a business trip, Cynthia and I stayed with a friend who assisted in placing children from southeast Asia. She asked me if anyone in South Australia would like to adopt two girls from Mauritius.

"They are old—11 and 12. Most folk won't take on the responsibility for children of that age," she said as she handed

Lori

me a paper with two small photos of Lori and Liseby. Their faces were somber and afraid, but something about their eyes touched my heart. I rang a number of people I thought might be interested in taking the girls into their families, but the answer was always the same, "Too old."

"Okay," I said to myself. "We can fit in a few more at our house."

When I called Keith from the road, he, ever the accountant, pointed out with some firmness that we already had ten children, and they were costing us a fortune. Nevertheless, by the time I arrived home two days later, and he saw the photos of the girls, their adoption became his own idea!

Making the decision to adopt was easy; getting the girls was not. We battled Australian bureaucracy for six months, finally taking our plight to the Minister of the Department of Community Welfare. When grudging approval from our government finally came, we prepared to welcome Lori and Liseby into our home, happily unaware of some very strange goings-on in Mauritius. As the months passed with no news of the girls' arrival, we became uneasy and exchanged increasingly frantic calls with our agent in Mauritius before we found out what had happened. To our incredulity, it seemed a jealous shaman—or witchdoctor—had, for reasons we could not even imagine, placed a spell on the girls. Each week, the adoption agency would take Lori and Liseby to the airport, only to turn back, convinced that the spell was still active. (It was only after the girls had been living with us for a good while that they confided that several attempts had been made on their lives during this waiting period.)

Each Saturday went the same way: "We got them to the airport, but had to take them back home." Eventually, the girls were isolated in a bare room for a week, with a mystic who rid them of this strange spell. When the call came, after six months, to say that the girls were on the weekly flight from Mauritius, we eagerly went to claim our new children.

Lori and Liseby fitted into our home without too much trauma and began school with their brothers and sisters very soon after arrival. They matured into lovely young women. Liseby, however, always seemed to carry a heavy burden on her shoulders. Kind, thoughtful and giving, she was always afraid of close personal contact and was reluctant to show her emotions. She seemed a loner. Just eleven years after her arrival in Australia, at twenty-four years of age, Liseby was diagnosed with cancer and passed away. "They finally got me," she said during her final days; that comment will always haunt me, referring, I believe, to the shaman in Mauritius.

Our family was devastated, and the pain of grief played heavily on our hearts. Our lives changed forever.

It was during the period of Liseby's illness that I began to quilt, mainly as an antidote to grief. One of the large quilts I made during that time is named "Liseby's Hope." It was my therapy as I watched my beautiful daughter struggle with her disease; my emotions were hidden in every stitch.

PART ONE

MY JOURNAL OF THE

1776 *Quilt*

Chapter 1

A Story of Heartache, Heritage, and Happiness

*I describe how my life followed
a winding path to 1776*

Liseby's Gift

The beginning of 1995 was a bleak time for me. Our daughter Liseby had died six months before, and I was in mourning for her. I knew my life had changed, and not for the better. I desperately needed to recover my good spirits since my son's wedding, which was to take place in Thailand, was fast approaching. When an invitation came from Liseby's close friend Rimi to spend some healing time with her in London, I accepted. (Rimi was an exchange student from Japan who stayed with us the year she and Liseby turned eighteen together.)

The trip to England marked the first time I had ever traveled alone, or even slept in a bedroom on my own. When you're the mother in a family of fifteen, there is always company. Loneliness, even time on one's own, never comes into the equation. As I set out for London, little did I know that this journey would set in motion a string of experiences that would change my life once again. When I look back, I think of the trip as Liseby's gift.

Upon arrival, I embarked on a ten-day bus tour of England—a whirlwind affair of eating, sight-seeing, and gazing through the windows of a tour bus, punctuated by short stops at obligatory tourist haunts. American accents

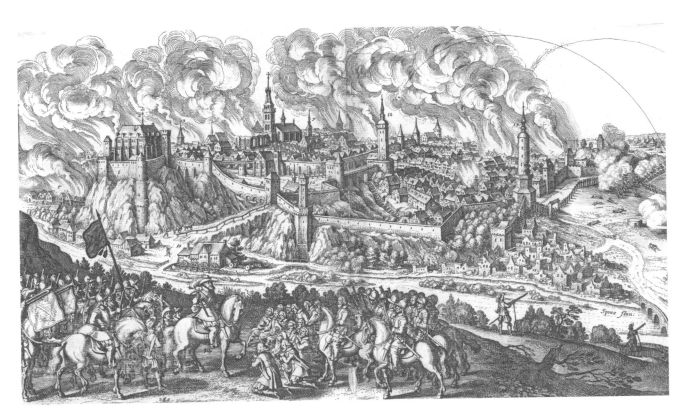

abounded, and I joined forces with Joan Dougherty, who described herself as "bog Irish American"; she had filled her large bag with tuna sandwiches, quilting magazines, and an assortment of fabrics. Meeting Joan turned out to be the highlight of the tour, and we became friends, as fabric lovers often do. Back in London, we would meet up to visit museums and other textile venues.

It was on one of our little jaunts that I purchased a book titled, simply, *Quilts.* Browsing through the pages, I came across a photograph of an old quilt made by European soldiers in 1776. This was my first encounter with an image that was to become an obsession with me. Back home, I enlarged the picture of the quilt for further inspection and found myself looking at it daily, even pulling out Grandpa's magnifying glass for a closer view. My personal odyssey began when I eventually made a decision to re-create the quilt.

A Journey of Discovery

I set out to draft the pattern for the quilt, working from my enlarged photo. I began with the center panel, an almost-square block with a sort of sunburst shape. I tried very hard to re-create the original exactly, but when one enlarges an eight-inch photo up to a nine-foot by ten-foot pattern, some of the details are lost! My diary records six different tries at making the center block. Needless to say, and as I was to find out, there is not one part of the quilt that can be considered a standard block. During my period of trial and error I tried to find out more about the quilt that had mesmerized me—*1776*.

Upon investigation, I traced the original quilt to a small museum in the ancient town of Bautzen in East Germany. Founded in 1002 as the main fort of an early Slavic people who are today known as Sorbs (more about them later), Bautzen was for thousands of years peacefully co-inhabited by Germans. By 1530, the city was owned by Czechoslovakia, and 100 years later, Bautzen was ceded to Saxony in the Peace of Prague.

As luck would have it, my husband and I had the opportunity to go to Europe in 2000. "Where would you like to go?" I asked him casually, with my fingers crossed behind my back.

"Oh, I don't mind, you choose." Of course, we headed for Germany, flying into Frankfurt. A further eight-hour train ride found us in Bautzen.

We arrived at a small brown train station bedecked with wooden seats, red geraniums, and old taxis. We showed an obliging taxi driver the piece of paper, written in German, with the name of the lodging we'd booked. He looked at us quizzically, piled the luggage into the back of the taxi, and ceremoniously drove us the one block to the hotel!

Our appointment with the museum director was for the next day, so we had an afternoon to explore. The town of Bautzen is situated on the River Spree, which ribbons through steep granite cliffs in a small valley of Upper Lusatia. There are four towers (each one different),

The picturesque city of Bautzen is rich in architectural detail dating back to the twelfth century. Perhaps some of the unusual motifs in the quilt were inspired by the town its soldier-creators called home.

which are connected by tall stone walls that have surrounded and protected the village for centuries. The walls managed to survive devastating city fires in 1709 and 1720.

Lusatia is the ancestral homeland of the Sorbs, a Slavic people who settled there nearly 1000 years ago. (The name "Lusatia" comes from a Sorbian word meaning swamp or waterhole.) The region is approximately fifty miles southeast of Berlin, about 1,800 square miles in area, and is bordered by Czechoslovakia on the south and Poland on the east. For more than ten centuries, the Sorbs have resisted assimilation into European cultures, maintaining their own language and customs. Despite the fact that Lusatia is also known as Sorbia, indicating their majority presence, Sorbs have not enjoyed political independence; they have been ruled at various times by Germans, Hungarians, Poles, and Bohemians.

In the year 1776, Sorbs made up one-fourth of Bautzen's population. Today there are only about 60,000 Sorbs left in the Lusatia, with approximately 40,000 of them in Bautzen—comprising about ten percent of the town's total population.

Bautzen (*Budissin* in Sorb) is, and has always been, the center of Sorbian culture. The city is considered a model of German/Sorbian relations, and the main statue in the town seeks to portray the embodiment of Sorbs and Germans living together. This is particularly relevant in view of the early treatment of Sorbs by the Germans who, from the twelfth and thirteenth centuries, viewed them as fit only for slavery. Sorbs were denied their civil rights unless they became completely integrated by abandoning their own culture and adopting Germany's. However, in today's Germany, Sorbs have certain minority rights, such as being able to send their children to Sorbian-language schools, use the Sorbian language in dealings with local governments, and use of bi-lingual road signs.

Keith and I meandered down narrow cobblestone streets built in the fourteenth century. We came upon the village square, once patron to markets and festivals, as well as to violent revolts, even hangings. The square was crowned with an intriguing clock and sundial in yet another tower. As we walked, we were transported back through history. The tall, brightly painted medieval houses seemed to greet us with smiles. Windows were dressed with boxes of colorful flowers.

The following day we arrived at the City Museum and duly presented our letter of introduction, only to find that the director, with whom we had an appointment, had taken the day off. No one spoke English or understood that we wanted to visit the quilt or anything else we said. Half an hour passed: at last, a young man arrived, running down the stairs to greet us in basic English. He was the janitor.

We were ushered upstairs and left alone. At last, I stood in front of 1776. Seeing it for the first time, I was overcome with emotion. I became short of breath and felt a strong urge to break down and cry. Finally, I was able to take out my camera. I photographed every inch of the quilt and closely investigated the intricacies of its workmanship.

In the time I stayed with the quilt, I was transported back to 1776. The soldiers and animals portrayed in the richly decorated blocks and panels had stood sentinel for 230 years. Who were their creators and what mysteries and stories were stitched into the quilt?

Stitching Soldiers

A bit of historical perspective on *1776* is offered by Schnuppe von Gwinner in *The History of the Patchwork Quilt*:

"A patchwork quilt in the same tradition of Silesian quilting still survives in the City Museum of Bautzen. It is sewn of uniform scraps of cloth [*Ed.* i.e., scraps of fabric from uniforms] and shows chessboard and star patterns, soldiers, Turks, miners, hunters and other patterns. The years 1776 and 1779 may stand for the beginning and end of the work or could also, considering the themes of the patterns, refer to a political connection. At this time the War of the Bavarian Succession took place, with

Prussian troops marching into Bohemia. The Peace of Teschen ended the war in 1779."

In 1776, the political climate of Lusatia, including its capital city of Bautzen, was a product of its rather complicated past. Over the centuries, the region had frequently changed hands between Saxony, Bohemia, and Brandenburg (which, between 1701 and 1947, was known as Prussia). All of Lusatia finally became part of Saxony in 1635, after which the strengthened Saxony formed various coalitions with Poland, Austria, and Prussia, always seeking partnerships that were to its greatest economic advantage, rather than those based on kinship or loyalty to a particular ruler.

At the time *1776* was made, the country was allied with Prussia.

Poland was in gradual decline, and Prussia had emerged as a major European power, hungry for expansion. When Bohemia was ceded to Austria, rather than to Germany, at the death of its duke (and the extinction of its major ruling family) in 1777, Prussia encouraged the heir presumptive of Bohemia to protest the way his lands were being divided, thereby encouraging the War of the Bavarian Succession. Prussia, assisted by Saxony, declared war on Austria in 1778 and invaded Bohemia. The war ended with the Congress of Teschen in 1779, with Prussia receiving Bavarian lands, and Saxony taking financial payments, in the settlement: no serious engagement ever took place. Indeed, the conflict was nicknamed the Potato War, because the pressure of battle was so minor that

Prussian troops occupied themselves by helping the local Saxon farmers harvest their potato crops.

If the Prussian soldiers had enough leisure to gather potatoes, it is easy to assume that they also had time for other pursuits such as stitchery. Just as the tedium of idle hours onboard ship led eighteenth-century sailors to occupy themselves with carving animal bones and teeth into the elaborate designs of scrimshaw, so did slack times on the battlefield compel soldiers to seek artistic outlets for their energies. Both groups of military men were limited by availability of materials, but that scarcity, it could be argued, was a stimulus to creativity. Worn-out uniforms and blankets provided most of the material for *1776*, and a great deal of its appeal lies in the way these plain, simple, unfigured, mostly solid-colored, woolen fabrics are manipulated into charming trees and flowers, prancing animals, and lively humans engaged in a variety of activities.

(One can even imagine the soldiers writing home to their wives, requesting fabrics for the quilt!)

Quilts with themes similar to *1776*, also made by soldiers around the same time period, exist in several European museums. One, a Bohemian bedcover from 1796 (thought to be in the collection of London's Victoria and Albert Museum, but currently unavailable for research or photography), exhibits many motifs similar to *1776*, and is worked in the same combination of patchwork and appliqué. Another similarity between the two quilts is their portrayal of the political situation of the times, when both countries,

Saxony and Bohemia, were expecting war to come at any moment. Who knows how many other quilts await discovery?

It was with a degree of sadness that I left the museum. As we wandered through the village, I felt an overwhelming sense of belonging, mentioning it several times to Keith. It was quite an eerie feeling, one that I talked about many times with my parents when I returned to Adelaide and recounted the story.

A Lost Technique Is Found Again

The original *1776* quilt was made from wool, which appeared to be felted, and was sewn from the back. Subsequent investigation has revealed that this method of construction is known as inlay quilting, and that it originated in Europe as early as the fifth or fourth century BC. Other examples demonstrate that the method was also used with silk fabrics.

How to execute the inlay quilting remains rather a mystery. A valiant attempt to explain it was made by Ulrike Telek, the director of textiles in the City Museum of Bautzen in her response to my inquiry, which I had to have translated from the original German. Even though Ms. Telek provided her own illustrations, I'm still not sure I understand the method.

"With this quilt you deal with *tuchintarsie—tuch* (cloth), *inarsie* (inlay). It consists of numerous pieces of fabric set together. To do this, the maker has used pieces of uniforms, woolen fabrics, made out of strong cord in weft and warp. Threads have been roughened after weaving and dying. Through this they are strong and firm enough to allow them to be worked as inlay. This is the way this quilt was made although it is an uncommon method.

'Examination of this technique has shown that all of the methods (listed below) have been used in this display of uniforms:

A letter from Director of the City Museum of Bautzen contains a description of how to accomplish inlay quilting.

1. Lay the pieces of cloth next to each other and sew in a simple sewing fashion—which was the custom for soldiers' uniforms.

2. Between the two fabrics vertical thin fabric stripes are sewn in different colors (like the piping on a uniform).

3. From pieces of cloth cut out particular motifs and, in a method similar to wooden inlay, lay them next to each other then sew from the back. This was a common method of adding decorations to uniforms.

4. Fine details are embroidered with silk thread.

'The quilt is finished with jute backing (a natural fiber similar to that used to make burlap or sacking).'

Scottish author Janet Rae in her book, *The Quilts of the British Isles*, perhaps explains the method more clearly:

"The inlay technique requires the fabric edges butt each other, and that the cloth used be thick enough to accommodate the oversewing required to hold the pieces in place. The over-sewing was done from the back with very fine stitches, which did not completely pierce the cloth, and the embroidery was decorative rather than functional."

Silesian Quilts

Following the advice of quilt expert Janet Rae, I visited the Glasgow Museum in Scotland to study three quilts that were constructed using the same basic method as the original 1776. Two of them are shown here.

The first quilt, The Royal Clothograph, was made by John Monroe, born in 1811, who became a tailor (and probably a maker of military uniforms) in the town of Paisley, Scotland. The quilt measures more than six-and-a-half feet square and took eighteen years to complete. It consists of a series of picture panels framed by mosaic images on fine black felted wool. Monroe embroidered the names of hundreds of famous men around the border, along with various pieties. Upon his death in 1888, the quilt was raffled to benefit his widow. Tickets went for one shilling each. (One shilling equals about ten cents, which was probably a considerable amount of money to pay for a raffle ticket in 1888.) A second quilt in the Glasgow Museum was also made by David Robertson in the year 1859 in the county of Falkirk, Scotland, and dis-

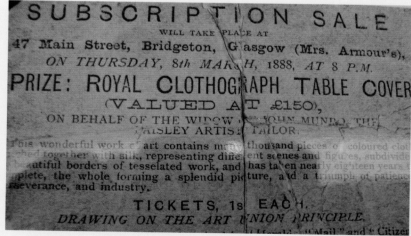

played a sailing ship.

There was also another wonderful quilt by David Robertson,

made in 1853 (not photographed). It is said that the quilt took Robertson 1,650 hours to complete.

AMERICAN CLIPPER SHIP·COBRA,
BY
DAVID ROBERTSON,
1859.

OPPOSITE TOP: The Royal Clothograph Quilt, made by John Monroe, "the Paisley Tailor." OPPOSITE BOTTOM: Upon his death, a raffle was held to benefit Monroe's widow; tickets were one shilling (ten cents) apiece. ABOVE: Details from David Robertson's sailing ship quilt.

A Passion Becomes an Obsession

While I had made attempts to draft patterns for my version of *1776* from a tiny photo as early as 1995, I did not start work on the quilt in earnest until the late 1990s. Following a year and a half of planning and preliminary work, I physically began making the quilt on Wednesday, 10 August, 1999. Stepping away from the original, I decided that I did not want to use wool for my re-creation. I did, however, want to follow the colors and patterns of *1776* as accurately as I could. I had a small collection of reproduction fabrics from the United States, and, lo and behold, many were reproductions of fabrics from the eighteenth century. The colors of these reproduction

fabrics were in harmony with those of the original quilt, so I added to my collection with my own purchases and with fabrics sent to me from friends in the United States.

My passion for the quilt became an obsession that saw the last stitch placed on 27 May, 2003—a total of 9586 hours, or 818 twelve-hour days. There are lots of stories associated with the making of the quilt—many sleepless nights, help of friends and family, days of 4:00 a.m. starts and midnight finishes. I worked methodically through the designing, drawing, appliquéing and piecing of each block, and I documented each step.

Some would say that this quilt is a copy. Indeed, one professional colleague puts it in that category, but I took ownership of the illustrations and designs of the blocks as the quilt grew. I choose to think that the quilt has been re-born through my eyes. I say the quilt has been re-created.

An Ending and a New Beginning

Although my recreation of this extraordinary quilt is finished, its story is not. The quilt has traveled around the world with me and has been honored at major quilt venues, particularly in the United States. (See Afterword on page 130 for more details.) I was deeply moved when my *1776* won Best in Show at International Quilt Market and Festival, held in Houston. In the following months, the quilt was to win awards in three other major US shows, as well as receive accolades of praise as I traveled with it in Europe and returned home to Australia. I was particularly gratified that the judges did not refer to the quilt as a copy or reproduction of an earlier design. It was considered as a new creation in its own right—and was to take on a life of its own as my teaching career developed.

I continue my search for other Silesian quilts, and am on the trail of several that are reported to be in Germany. I would very much like to take my quilt to Bautzen, Germany, to share it with the citizens of the town who made the original *1776*. My dream is to see the two quilts hang side by side in an exhibition.

Call it coincidence or fate, there is one more important story to tell in connection with *1776*. In August 2001 my mother telephoned. With a tremor in her voice, she told me that she had just returned from a family funeral in South Kilkerran, a country town three hours

from Adelaide, South Australia. Mother, now in her 70s, had been visiting with distant cousins, uncles, and aunts, and was told the history of her family for the first time. Her grandfather, Carl Augustas Elies, had arrived in Australia in 1884. He belonged to a religious sect known as the Moravian Brethren. He was of Sorbian descent and came to Australia from the area of Bautzen and Goerlitz, with a few other families from the same religious group. As I grew up, I was very close to my grandfather, Carl Augustas Elies' son. Not only had I dedicated the quilt to him, but the pattern I called "Elies' block" was designed in his honor.

To me, the fact that my great-grandfather was a Sorb from Bautzen explains my passion for *1776*. It also explains the peculiar sense of belonging that I had experienced when viewing the quilt in my great-grandfather's hometown. Further, I believe that my daughter Liseby gave me the opportunity to visit England, which led to my introduction to the original quilt. For me, my recreation of that antique quilt is a testament to Liseby's life, and she lives on through the quilt. Had we not lost her, I would not have discovered quiltmaking, nor would my career as a quilter have ever reached the heights that I am now experiencing. This is why the quilt and this book that is based upon it could bear but one name: *The 1776 Quilt: Heartache, Heritage, and Happiness.*

Chapter 2

Journaling the Quilt

*I explain why I needed a personal record
and describe my sewing environment and the
tools I used to create my 1776*

I have kept a journal for the past 30 years. Some years it is quite sparse, other years quite detailed, even to the extent of including such memorabilia as theater tickets, shopping lists, cards, and drawings done for me by the children. Every couple of years I make a pot of coffee, sit down for a few hours, and relive the past by leafing through my journals. Most of the events I have recorded make me laugh, because I always see the funny side of things. We have had our share of sadness, too, and those memories are painful to recall. However, the journals always remain the same—never changing. They rest there in the bookcase, full of memories.

As a child, I was a passionate Norman Rockwell fan. I would sit for hours and gaze at his paintings on the covers of the *Saturday Evening Post*. He portrayed everyday life. He turned the mundane into a story with humor and poignancy, and that is what I try to do with my journals.

During the making of the *Liseby's Hope* quilt, I kept a separate journal just for the quilt. It was my way of expressing our sorrow at the journey our daughter traveled and its impact on our family. I liken the journal to a ripple in a pond. Those who read it are made aware of the

rings of sadness that radiated from that event. The quilt is a tactile reminder, while the journal is a word picture.

Even though I had journaled only that one quilt project previous to *1776*, I knew from the outset that the making of this quilt was something that I should document for my family. I had found through that one occurrence that keeping a journal during the making of a quilt allowed me later to relive the artistic experience (albeit in a conveniently smaller capsule of time). It was very rewarding to review the entire creative process once the quilt was finished.

I recorded my honest and innermost feelings as I struggled with the complexities of creating *1776*. I know that if I am completely and ruthlessly truthful in my journal, I will record for all time the difficulties, as well as the triumphs, of the process. This is important because, upon completion of a wholly original quilt design, I can get lost in the beauty of the finished product and easily forget the details of the problems I solved along the way, all the trials and errors, the stops and starts. I can also fail to remember the utter determination it took to accomplish the project. That is why I would suggest that any quilt journal you keep should reflect what actually happened, rather than an idealized version of the experience—the truth is more satisfying in the long run.

Although the journal entries in the chapters that follow are basically as I wrote them, some passages have been shortened to save space and avoid repetition; a few have been edited for clarity. (I did not imagine that the journal would be published, so I wrote only for myself, not with the goal of communicating to others. Consequently, a bit of clearing up was necessary here and there.)

No entries have been deleted, although there is no consistency in their dating. I didn't write in the journal every day, and at times several weeks, even several months, passed between journal entries. Some interruptions were due to situations that came up within the family, opportunities for fun and excitement, and others are attributable to the heavy teaching schedule I kept. The idea is to enjoy journaling, not to become a slave to it.

My Environment

I am always interested in the different settings in which people make their quilts, so I will tell you about mine. I am fortunate enough to have a studio, known as "The Shed", where I can work on a project and leave it spread out without risk of being disturbed, nor having it interfere with normal family life. The Shed, completely separate from my house, is made of galvanized tin and measures 30 feet by 20 feet. It is very similar to those buildings in backyards across America that contain gardening equipment or woodworking tools. However, my shed houses my computers, sewing machines, cutting tables and, of course, a significant stash of fabric. It is a gathering place for visitors—quilters and non-quilters alike—as well as family. Over the years, I have added a small veranda, complete with bird feeders for the beautiful array of birds that visit each day. The porch also serves as a roosting spot for my covey of domestic white doves.

My Equipment

People are alway curious about the tools and materials I used to construct 1776, and I wonder if they are not sometimes disappointed to find that no rare and exotic methods or resources figure in my work. Over the years I have established a preference for certain materials and equipment, and there were a few specific items required for this particular quilt. See Resources on page 163 for more information about individual products.

COMPUTER

My computer is my most important tool as a quilt designer. I use it to design the overall quilt, to draw my appliqués, to try out different colors, and to design fabric. One of the first things I am asked when I talk about 1776 is the complexity of the pattern—how did I figure it out? The computer was a great help.

FABRIC

Although I incorporated into the quilt fabrics from many different manufacturers, such as Kaufmann, Benartex, and others, the ones that most closely match the colors of the original quilt are from Cherrywood. They are hand-dyed and appear to have been put through some kind of process to age the colors. The subtle shadings match the wonderful colors in the reproduction eighteenth-century fabrics that I bought from other sources.

I also used some Amish-type colors for the background of the next-to-last appliqué border (a series of different-color squares displaying

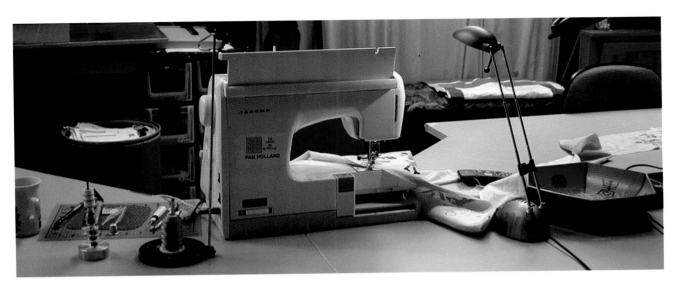

various folk motifs). They fit wonderfully into the quilt. I feel that, since mine is a quilt of the twenty-first century, it is all right to use some twenty-first century fabrics—I don't feel the need to limit the palette to just eighteenth-century reproduction fabrics.

QUILT BATTING

I prefer Warm and Natural® batting because it is thin, 100 percent cotton, and the quilting design shows up beautifully. My quilts are always used as wall hangings and I want them to lie flat against the wall. A batting with a higher loft—such as wool or polyester—will yield a different effect, and I personally don't think it looks as attractive suspended on the wall. Save those battings for lap or bed quilts.

APPLIQUÉ ESSENTIALS

Heat-sensitive fabric adhesives are a great help in appliqué. Also known as fusible web, there are many excellent choices available to quilters in the United States; in Australia, I choose Vliesofix®, which originates in Germany.

Appliqué mats or sheets are essential for working with fusibles, especially when, as in the Elies block (see pages 65 to 66), it becomes necessary to apply fusible interfacing to the back of a quilt piece that has a hole in it. Appliqué mats and sheets do not melt when a hot iron is applied, and they do not accept the heat-sensitive resins used to make fusible webs and fabrics, so the resins remain on the web or fabric. I use a Teflon® appliqué mat that began life as a baking sheet. A clever quilter figured out it could be used as an appliqué mat, and I highly recommend it for every quilter's basic tool kit.

I always lay out all the pieces for a particular design on an appliqué mat before I begin to sew–just to make sure the colors are how I want them.

Stabilizers, placed behind a fabric, are very helpful in creating intricate appliqué shapes. Without a stabilizer, the lightweight cotton fabrics used in quilts can become puckered when intricate and heavy appliqué stitches are applied. I use a thin, woven cotton product named Quilt Lite® from Freudenburg, the same company that makes Vliesofix®. (In some areas of *1776* that were heavily stitched, I used three layers of this stabilizer to support the surface fabric.) A comparable product in the United States is Quilt Light® by Mountain Mist®.

Some stabilizers are fusible, especially some paper and tear-away ones. However, all paper stabilizers, fusible or not, should be torn away after stitching is completed, and that can be very time-consuming. I am also concerned that any residue of paper that remains in the quilt will have an adverse affect on the quilt as it ages. My preference is for a woven cotton stabilizer with a natural tendency to cling to the surface fabric, eliminating the need for fusing, such as Quilt Lite® and Quilt Light®.

THREADS AND NEEDLES

Different types of threads and needles are required for different techniques.

For appliqué, in order to get a truly professional finish, thread must match fabric color exactly. I prefer to use a fine (size 60) lingerie thread in rayon, polyester, silk or cotton, and especially like a thread made by Superior, called The Bottom Line®, because it comes in many colors.

For piecing or sewing sections together, the thread I use is grey, because it is a good neutral color, and of cotton, because it is strong.

My machine embroidery is almost always done with gold metallic thread. It requires a Metafil® needle, which has a larger eye especially to accommodate short staple rayon, and metallic, threads. The Metafil® needle eye is designed and polished to prevent snagged and broken threads.

For machine quilting, I like to use a tri-lobal polyester, rayon, or silk thread, because all are fine and feed easily through the slender needle I like to use, plus they have a sheen that makes them show up well on the quilt. However, fine threads are not the only choice; you can use any thickness you want. Whatever thread you choose, ensure an even stitch by using it in both the bobbin and the top threading of the machine. Again, I favor The Bottom Line® by Superior.

The needle I prefer for machine quilting is small: size 60/8 sharp or 70/10. With a sharp needle and fine thread both on the top and in the bobbin, I can get a very even quilting stitch. (I love the way the needle goes through the three layers, just like a hot knife through butter.)

Chapter 3

And So It Begins

I describe how I drafted patterns and took my first stitches, making everything from simple appliqué hearts to my favorite design, Elies block

First Steps

As I read over the journal entries I made while making the quilt, I remember how completely engrossed I was in everything I was doing. All my days of trial and error are recorded here and, looking back, I am sometimes amazed at how tough it was for me to puzzle out the quite complicated designs in 1776. I had only made a few quilts before I began this project, and I was to find that I was at the beginning of a rather steep learning curve. I didn't always replicate details precisely. Most noticeably, I worked hard to "square" the quilt, taking care that I would be able to sew blocks together evenly and count on having symmetrical borders. At times, the mathematics involved made my head spin. The soldier-creators of the original quilt did not worry themselves too much with symmetry or exact alignments, but their quilt has an easy grace that only increased as their colors faded with the passing of time.

WEDNESDAY, 10 AUGUST, 1999

I'm about to cut and stitch the center block, which I designed using Electric Quilt 4. I will have to make it up in several different ways to see which technique will work best. First I need to piece the background of triangles, then I'll appliqué the center circle with the hearts over the background.

It's not working! Nevertheless, it wasn't a waste of time. I was able to view the blend of colors, and I am quite happy with the fabrics I've chosen. However, it's not sitting correctly; the points don't seem to meet accurately at the center. And, even though the center will be covered with an appliquéd circle, I feel as though the points should be perfect underneath it. It's just so frustrating.

I have now printed the block from the computer onto material I use for paper piecing, with the hope that a different technique will help. However, I am going to first try piecing the block with templates one more time.

It's 4:25 p.m., and I've worked on this one block all day. I only took time off for lunch, and now I need to prepare tea. It has been really trying. My second template-pieced block didn't work either, because, as I finally discovered, I had drafted the block on the computer incorrectly.

Next, I went to the foundation pattern I had printed out earlier in the day and made a third sample. Oh darn, this one was incorrect as well—something with the proportion. At last, I returned to the computer, took an existing block from the EQ4 library, manipulated it, and—JOY!—it is correct. Now I'm going to complete it by hand. I hope the fourth time is lucky!

THURSDAY, 11 AUGUST, 1999

I got up quite early and took another look at the last center block I made yesterday. Something was still off with the proportion.

I figured I could machine-piece it accurately, so I made another block. Breakfast had to wait. This was attempt number five, and I was reasonably satisfied with the results. However, I decided to enlarge the center circle (with the hearts) and machine-appliqué it onto the background of triangles.

I had little time to work on the quilt today, because I gave a talk about quilting to a group of year-eleven students at Kildare College. I'm not too sure what they all thought, but some of them seemed to enjoy it. (Actually, I had more response from my daughter Rachael's year-four class when I spoke to them.)

In the evening I worked on the computer, designing blocks for the many borders and sizing them to the quilt. It took some time, but I finally figured out how to fit the required number of blocks into each border.

I spent my time today going through the drawings for the appliqué of the central panel. I drew the figures onto fusible web and tidied the fabrics for easier use. Goodness knows how long they will stay like that.

I think I have enough fabric to complete the blocks. Sometimes the combination of fabrics makes me feel uncomfortable, but I want to make my re-creation as much like the original as possible, so I just grit my teeth!

Absolute Joy: Deciphering Elies Block

MONDAY, 16 AUGUST, 1999

Great excitement! I received a letter today from the Bautzen museum! Now I just have to find someone to translate it for me.

This is an absolute joy! I placed the appliqué hearts onto the center of the panel! I have to say that the yellow hearts on the mustard feels very uncomfortable, but I'm attempting to stick as close to the original colors as possible.

I suddenly realized that I have to re-do the drawings in reverse to place them onto fusible web, since the web goes on the wrong side of the fabric. If I don't do them in reverse, they will be going in the wrong direction on the actual block. The hearts and dots are fine, because they have no direction, but the rest need to be reversed. (Note: For complete information on my appliqué method, see pages 62 to 63 and page 67.)

Each time a letter came from Germany, I had to find a translator. This is one of the later letters I received from Ulrike Telek, the Director of Textiles at the City Museum of Bautzen.

REGIONALMUSEUM DER SÄCHSISCHEN OBERLAUSITZ
REGIONALNY MUZEJ SAKSKEJE HORNJEJE ŁUŽICY

PAR AVION

Pam Holland
P.O. Box 11,
Aldgate 5154
South Australia

STADT
MUSEUM
BAUTZEN

MĚŠĆANSKI MUZEJ BUDYŠIN
DATUM   30.09.2003
AKTENZEICHEN
POSTFACHADRESSE
POSTFACH 1109   02601 BAUTZEN
HAUSADRESSE
KORNMARKT 1   02625 BAUTZEN
VERWALTUNG
KESSELSTRASSE 34   02625 BAUTZEN
TELEFON   (0 35 91) 49 85-0
TELEFAX   (0 35 91) 49 85 40
INTERNET www.bautzen.de
E-MAIL   stadtmuseum@bautzen.de

Sehr geehrte Pam Holland,

für Ihren Brief vom 25. August 2003 und den Ausdruck des Fleckenteppichs danken wir Ihnen. Über die Geschichte des Teppichs ist nichts bekannt. Zur Technik erhielten Sie bereits früher einige Informationen. Wir können Ihnen mitteilen, daß sich in den Städtischen Sammlungen für Geschichte und Kultur Görlitz, Postfach 30 01 31, 02806 Görlitz ähnliche Teppiche befinden.
Auch diese Objekte sind aus Tuch und in gleicher Technik gearbeitet.
Im Sorbischen Museum Bautzen ist die Geschichte der Sorbischen Auswanderer vor kurzem in einer Ausstellung gezeigt worden. Vielleicht können Sie dort die gewünschten Informationen erhalten, Sorbisches Museum, Ortenburg 3, 02625 Bautzen.

Mit freundlichen Grüßen

Ulrike Telek
Wissenschaftliche Mitarbeiterin

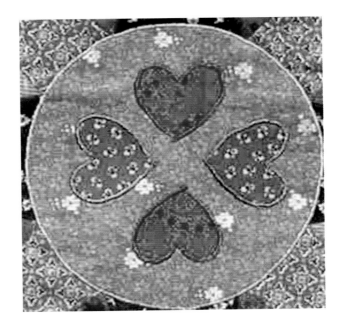

TUESDAY, 17 AUGUST, 1999

I spent the morning putting the appliqué onto the center block. I finally broke down and DID IT! I changed the yellow hearts in the center; I just couldn't cope with yellow on mustard. I wonder why they used those colors? I have decided that, after all, this is *my* quilt, and I will change it as I see fit to please myself. Now I'm really thrilled with the block, even though it has taken me almost a week of experimenting to get it right. I can complete an entire quilt in that time, but I want this quilt to be perfect. It's a challenge for me and one of those things I just have to do.

The pair of yellow hearts in the original quilt just didn't appeal to me, and I made them blue in my quilt.

SAME DAY

Now I need to make the surrounding blocks, the "Elies" blocks. The name comes from my grandfather, Reinhardt Elies, to whom I was very close. Since this is not a standard quilt block, I decided I could name it in his honor. To make the finished Elies block, I must make "Hourglass" blocks in two different sizes, then cut the top, four-petal shape out of one and appliqué it over the other. (Note: Complete step-by-step instructions for making the Elies block are on pages 65 to 66. Use them, not this journal entry, for making your own Elies blocks.)

I have made up two perfect 4 ½" Hourglass blocks, only to find they are not exactly what I need. It looks like I'm going to have to cut each triangle and every appliqué shape separately, but I'm concerned that I won't be able to get the corners of the appliqué shape to match. After a lot of trial and error, I have made up some samples.

Using the technique for making half-square triangles, I made another set of perfect 4 ½" Hourglass blocks, beginning with two 5 ½" squares of fabric and cutting the finished block to size. I repeated the technique, using two 4" squares, to make a 3" block.

Because the seams of the Hourglass blocks would create unmanageable bulk, especially at the center, if they were stacked, I cut away a section of the center from the 4 ½" square, which is the base of the Elies block. I then fused a square of lightweight iron-on interfacing onto the back of the resulting open-centered square. Next, I traced the four-petal shape for the center onto a piece of fusible web, fused it to the back of the 3" Hourglass block, cut out the four-petal shape, removed the paper, and fused the shape on top of the 4 ½" block. I found that, not only does the iron-on interfacing on the back of the larger block prevent the fusible web on the small block from sticking to the ironing board, it also acts as an additional bonding agent for the smaller block.

This seems quite a cumbersome approach to making the block, but I can't see any other way. I appliquéd the block first in satin stitch and then I tried another in blanket stitch, both with a gold thread. The blanket stitch set at a 2.0 stitch width, 2.0 stitch length on my Janome 9000 machine. (On a Bernina, the equivalent stitch width is about 1.4.) It is done with gold Raiman rayon thread (Number 121) on top and the same color in the bobbin. I tried both buttonhole and blanket stitches to see which would give me the effect I wanted. My goal was to have the embroidery duplicate the look of the wool piping used in the original quilt. A buttonhole stitch proved too difficult to apply over the many seam-lines of the Elies block; the blanket stitch was much more forgiving; it was possible to achieve a smooth outline in the areas I wanted to accent.

WEDNESDAY, 18 AUGUST, 1999
Spent some time typing up my journal.

TUESDAY, 22 AUGUST, 1999
There are three processes in making the Elies block. But, after a week or two of thinking about it and trying various methods, I'm satisfied with the results.

I've made the block ⅛" larger to allow me to cut it back to the correct size of 4 ½" finished. I'll leave the blocks as they are for now, and trim them when I'm ready to put them together. I only fully completed four Elies blocks today, but I made twenty Hourglass blocks in preparation for more.

TUESDAY, 31 AUGUST, 1999
I completed eight Elies blocks and the appliqué of the center block. The appliqué was done on the Janome 9000 in a buttonhole stitch: length, 1.5, going down to .05; and width, .35.

I pulled a section of the second row of Elies blocks apart because I wasn't happy with the balance of the colors. I can't help myself; everything has to be in line, in order, and balanced. I think there is a syndrome associated with this need for balance in everything.

Finally, at 7:34 p.m., after a hot and tiring day, I have made and sewn together Round Number Two of the Elies blocks. I took a long time aligning the blocks; with the 45° angles, there are *sixteen thicknesses* of fabric in the seams.

Rare it is to discover a completely new patch work block, but this one appears to be unique to the original *1776* quilt. I named it after my grand-father, Reinhart Elies. I tried seeing how the top shape would look on point (left), but decided to use the same placement as the original (right).

The Notch blocks in the four corners of this border are different from any other patchwork block I have ever seen; between the Notch and the Elies blocks, this old quilt has yielded a pair of totally new patchwork designs. (See pages 68 to 69 for directions to make the Notch block.) I don't work on this quilt at night because it is too difficult to choose the correct colors.

Checkerboards and Borders

WEDNESDAY, 29 SEPTEMBER, 1999

My father's 79th birthday.

I have just drawn up six blocks for the narrow border that surrounds each of the four checkerboards. This border is only 2" wide, and there are 106 different appliqué motifs in it! Oiy!

At the moment I don't have a suitable red fabric for the checkerboard and I need to give it more thought.

I wonder what the significance of the checkerboard is? Does it indicate that the soldiers had time on their hands, and that they played checkers to while some of it away? Was it perhaps a reminder of home and the finer things that home brings? Or was it a symbol of a masculine pastime, in which one man pitted his brains against another to see who was the better strategist?

TUESDAY, 19 OCTOBER, 1999

Back at home after two weeks away for the school holidays, I finally have a day to work on the quilt.

Yesterday I purchased the fabric for the checkerboard, a solid "turkey" red and a cream from the "Documentaries" line by Benartex. I think I will make the easier checkerboard first—it has slightly fewer appliqués in the border. (That is the red-and-cream one.) I need to make two red-and-cream and two navy-and-red checkerboards.

I cut four red and four cream strips 1 ½" wide across the width of the fabric. I think I should be able to make three blocks out of that. I need only two blocks in each colorway, but I would like to make another one for a sample quilt. There are so many wonderful blocks in this quilt, my mind runs rampant with ideas for smaller pieces utilizing these motifs. (See the projects in Part Three.)

THURSDAY, 25 JANUARY, 2001

There is a huge storm raging outside, the heavens have opened, lightning is flashing, and the clouds are releasing much needed rain. It has been hot, with average temperatures in the 30s (Celsius—high 80s Fahrenheit) for the past month, making it difficult to work on the project. However, last night I worked late into the evening, preparing the small appliqué dots and placing them on the checkerboard block. It doesn't look like much, but they are fiddly and need to be placed accurately or the block will be out of balance.

I think I will appliqué them in invisible thread. My reason for doing so is to allow the edge of the circle to be seen and remain round. If I use satin stitch in regular thread, it is difficult to maintain the pure circle.

I trimmed the block back to 12" and find that I will need to fudge a little on the top and bottom. The sides are correct but I'm just a little short the other direction. I need to make sure that I don't allow that to happen when I do the next two checkerboards.

SATURDAY, 27 JANUARY, 2001

Got up early this morning and made the trek to Office Works to get some supplies for the class beginning on Monday. At the same time I purchased some hard-to-find Schmetz sharps, size 60/8. They are ideal machine needles for invisible appliqué.

So I began appliquéing the very small dots on the checkerboard border. I find that I get a much better finish with the finer needle and matching bobbin thread. For the pale blue, I used clear monofilament and a white bobbin thread.

TUESDAY, 30 JANUARY, 2001

It's 6:30 a.m., and I am beginning to cut the strips for the second two checkerboard blocks, using blue fabric I purchased in 1997 from Cherrywood. It is very similar to the color in the original block, and looks good with the turkey red. Strips are cut 1 ½" wide and sewn with a ¼" seam.

I think that these two checkerboards are going to be slightly larger than the first set. I kept an accurate ¼" seam, but the first lot seemed smaller, so I made another set, allowing a little more space.

I drew and cut out the appliqués and applied them to the block. There are 120 individual pieces on the second, blue-and-red set of checkerboards (14 more than on the red-and-cream ones).

The checkerboard blocks themselves were simple; it was the borders, with more than 100 different appliqués, that were tedious to make!

Time Marches On: The Hourglass Border

THURSDAY, 1 FEBRUARY, 2001

Well, the panic has set in. I have given myself the task of completing this project before I travel on the 13 May. Can I do it?

Looking back on this diary I see that I have taken a week to make two blocks and appliqué another. Admittedly I spent Sunday completing a class project and yesterday was S&B (Stitch & Bitch), but I need to push myself—maybe even work out what I can do each day. I also feel the need to walk for an hour each day to get much-needed exercise after sitting at the machine all day. The problem is that it is so hot at the moment.

Today I have completed as much of the appliqué as I can without the correct thread. Tomorrow I will take the fabric into the city to get matching thread. I'm anxious to complete the next round, and already my head is spinning. I want to surge ahead but the amount of work makes it impossible.

I need to document what I am doing accurately every day and put it onto CD for fear of losing it.

It was hot today, about 39°C (102°F) here in the shed. I got a small fan, beamed it on my face, and was quite comfortable. I have appliquéd quite a bit of the border for the checkerboards, but I have the small dots to complete. I did put the stars on the appliqué, but they were too big, so I need to go back to the drawing board and make them smaller. I had stuck them on, but, fortunately, it was so hot the glue hadn't stuck effectively, and they were easy to remove.

After twelve straight hours of appliqué, I decided to make the Hourglass blocks that surround the center part of the quilt. At 7:00 p.m. I stopped appliquéing and made up 26 Hourglass blocks. I just need to trim them tomorrow.

FRIDAY, 2 FEBRUARY, 2001

I was out here at 6:30 this morning and trimmed the Hourglass blocks to 4 ½". I didn't do it last night, because I was tired, and sometimes when I'm tired I make mistakes. The temperature is already very high, but I need to go to a valuation meeting for the South Australian Quilt Guild, and then to buy Jinda's new uniform. (The Guild's valuation committee meets once a month to value quilts for its members; I have been on the committee for several years.) I will take the opportunity to purchase more threads as well. I'm suffering from an inner ear infection and my balance is affected.

In considering the colors to use in the appliqué of the soldiers, I have decided to use Cherrywood fabric, so I will look at the colors I have, select what I need, and purchase matching threads for the soldiers today too.

It has been wonderful to have close-up photos of the quilt. I have printed a lot of them out and put them in my workbook. I can refer back to them as needed. It is amazing just how detailed the appliqué is when you look at it closely.

PHOTOGRAPHIC JOURNAL

When writing my journal during the years I made *1776*, I had no thoughts of future publication. I had no idea how interested quilters would be in my re-creation of the original Bautzen quilt, and so I kept the journal for my own sake, not for a general readership. The same was true of the photographs I took during the process. Most of the photographs in Part One of this book were from my own camera. That includes most of the travel shots of

My faithful companion, Tenterfield terrier Ralf, takes a rest on a pile of Hourglass blocks that had slipped to the floor in one of my sewing frenzies.

Bautzen and all the photographs taken in and around my studio. It also includes the shots of the original quilt, which I took at the museum when I first saw the quilt on display. I tried to photograph every section in detail, so that I could use the shots while working on my quilt.

When the manuscript was ready for publication, my publisher received some very bad news. The museum at Bautzen was closed for renovation, and *1776* was no longer available to be photographed. Rather than delay the book, we made the decision to move ahead using my original photographs. Since the quality of the images is not ideal, most are reproduced at a size that makes a compromise between image quality and the reader's desire to see color and detail.

Chapter 4

Soldiering On

I complete hundreds of appliqués, tackle the borders, and defeat moments of desperation as deadlines approach

Time Out

Time got away from me after I had completed the center portion of my version of *1776*, and more pressing matters led me to set the project aside. In short, the need to earn a living got in the way of my desire to work on the quilt. A busy teaching schedule, the writing of patterns, and my usual hectic family life all played their part. I had my first taste of success during this "missing year," though, when one of my quilts won a notable award. I knew then that *1776* would be a most unusual quilt and began to wonder how it would be received by the quilting community.

MONDAY, 28 JANUARY, 2002

I can't imagine that it has been an entire year since I picked up my *1776* quilt. I have missed it; it is so special to me and is constantly in my mind. I had to pack it away the first of February, 2001, to go on the back burner while I've had one of the best years I've ever experienced.

I put *1776* aside to complete a project I named *Folk Art Rose of Sharon*. It was a huge success and won an award in Japan. I love the quilt, and I learned a lot about design and technique as I made it—it was a good test piece for the *1776* quilt.

Before I took a year's sabbatical from *1776*, I had made and bordered the center square and the checkerboards, and I had quantities of Hourglass blocks ready to be made into borders or used in Elies blocks. This detail shows a favorite but challenging motif from one of the appliqué borders I was yet to begin.

Then, I spent six months teaching in the United States and Japan, during which time I was awarded the prestigious Jewel Pearce Patterson Scholarship for international quilt teachers by the International Quilt Market and Festival in Houston.

Also, I have spent a considerable amount of time preparing and sending out patterns. My patterns have to take precedence, since they are income-producing. However, here I am again ready to go! I'm excited.

Today I began the 6½" Elies blocks that will eventually be used in side borders. I need twenty of these blocks in all. The formula: cut twenty 7½" squares, make ten Hourglass blocks, which, when trimmed and combined, convert to twenty 6½" Elies blocks. I also need twenty 4½" Hourglass blocks for the center, so I cut twenty 5½" squares and proceeded as for the 6½" blocks.

I managed to sew a sample block and cut just five blocks before succumbing to exhaustion, after a really long day here in the shed.

TUESDAY, 29 JANUARY, 2002

3:00 a.m., and I am completing those twenty Elies blocks. It is such a long process. Really, you need to make forty blocks and appliqué them at the same time, so you are doing three times the amount of work. However, I love this block; it is so unique and so different from any other I have ever seen.

I work slowly and accurately, because, ultimately, it saves time. Once I make the central four-petal shape and appliqué it to the block, I then have enough space on the block to trim it back to 7". Oh no, I just measured it—it barely measures 6¾"! I need it to be 7", so it will end up 6½" in the quilt. Jeepers. Oh well, I will finish these, and put them in the box for another day and begin all over again. Hmmm.

Maybe I will use these undersized blocks for the centers of the larger Elies blocks. I will waste some fabric, but it will save me time. Problem solved. They look just gorgeous.

These are the last of the pieced blocks that I need to make for the quilt, the rest of the quilt is all appliqué, and lots of borders, sixteen in all, I think. I purchased some wonderful fabric at the Lowell Museum and the Shelburne Museum and, as these are the final pieced

Playing with Design

When I first looked at the original *1776* in detail, I was fascinated by the Elies block. It was so unusual and the combination of shapes intrigued me. I began to experiment with it and came up with a series of designs that were created simply by rotating and repositioning multiple Elies blocks. The pattern shown here is one of my favorites. I also began playing with the Notch block, and came up with a design for that, too. These quilt details show how much fun I had with the designs. I used few colors, since I wanted to emphasize the distinct shapes of the Notch and Elies blocks when they were arranged in different ways. When I shared *1776* with my quilting friends, they, too, picked up on these particular designs. If you look at some of the "offspring" quilts in Part Three, you will see how different designers treated the block. I love Dianne Assheton's treatment in *The Four Horsemen*—a detail of that quilt is shown here. As a teacher, one of the most exciting aspects of my job is to see how other quilters work with colors and shapes to create entirely different effects that I am able to myself.

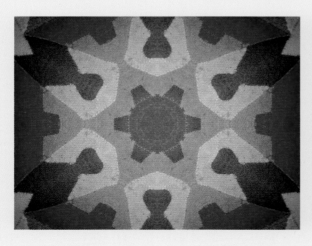

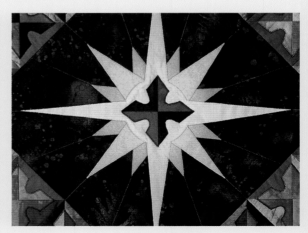

blocks, I put every bit of it into the quilt. It is a real adventure when you put colors and patterns together that you wouldn't normally use. When each new Hourglass block emerges, I love every one.

I worked for eight hours today on the large Elies blocks, amidst cleaning the shed and painting the walls.

WEDNESDAY, 30 JANUARY, 2002

I got up early and made twenty blocks for the base of the second set of Elies blocks. However, I had a visit to the city for Jinda's school interview, so I only worked for two hours today.

THURSDAY, 31 JANUARY, 2002

The center of the large Elies blocks should be 4½", so I would have had to make twenty 5" Hourglass blocks for the center four-petaled appliqué. And I made a mistake and made the Hourglass blocks too large—6½." In fact, just what am I thinking? I check, re-check and still make mistakes.

Up early and I have just completed tracing the new blocks. I have decided that I will use the "mistake" blocks from yesterday to make twenty extra blocks for a new and different project. I really can't waste them. I can take advantage of the mistake by covering the entire back of the 6½" Hourglass block with fusible web, then carefully cutting away the inside for those four-petal shaped images needed for the center part of my large Elies blocks.

There are a total of 94 Elies blocks in the quilt. Although most of them—those in the center of the quilt—are 4" square, the ones in the outer side borders of the central panel are larger—6." That means that I actually had to make 188 Hourglass blocks, because, as we know by now, two are required for each single Elies block.

Family Ties and the Appliqué Borders

MONDAY, 4 FEBRUARY, 2002

I had a great day yesterday with Mum and Dad. We talked about my grandfather, whose family came to this country after suffering religious persecution as Moravian Brethren. We looked at the book on Bautzen and talked at length about family history.

I began work this morning at 4:30 a.m., and completed appliquéing the final 6" Elies blocks. I find I have made two more than I need, so I will keep them as samples.

I am now able to move on to the next two borders of the quilt.

FRIDAY, 15 MARCH, 2002

Such a long time between work days—almost six weeks. However, we had a wonderful trip to Chile in the interim to attend the wedding of our daughter Yvette. We have been home a week, and I am now back to working on the quilt.

It has taken me an entire day to draw and assemble the lower appliqué panel that runs below the checkerboard blocks; it and the corresponding top panel are not identical. It is the first appliqué panel in the quilt, and I find the stylized trees and plants really interesting. I believe the animals are deer.

I have kept as close as possible to the original colors, but it has taken a considerable amount of time to assemble just this one section of the border.

WEDNESDAY TO THURSDAY, 21 TO 22 MARCH, 2002

Although I haven't documented it, I have been working on the quilt for the past few days. It has actually taken me four days to prepare the appliqué for the four borders. I decided to assemble them first and then appliqué them all together. It will take me a week to appliqué them, I think.

The side borders are really a challenge. The shape (which I later named *pomegranate* is difficult to appliqué, because of the points at the end. I need to get them as sharp as possible, because three of them come together at each end.

The pomegranate motifs will be 4" long, in order to keep them in line with the pieced Hourglass blocks of the preceding row. Because the width of the background strip on which the pomegranates are placed is only 3," the pomegranates can be no wider than 2 ¼"—fortunately, this creates a nice proportion for the oval shape. It is challenging to place the appliqués accurately so that the ends of each pomegranate match exactly the seamlines of the Hourglass block. (See also page 74.) To make the process easier, I first assembled the three sections of each appliqué oval by fusing them to lightweight non-woven iron-on interfacing, using the heatproof craft sheet. I pressed a positioning line down the center of the border strip, then placed the pieces on the line.

MONDAY, 1 APRIL, 2002

It has taken ten days to complete this first appliqué border. And as I look at the quilt, I am having heart failure and despairing that I won't get it finished. However, I had to take at least three days to prepare my submission for teaching in Houston (at the International Quilt Market and Festival), and that took a considerable amount of time from my appliquéing adventures.

Easter was a blessing—four days to myself (no phones or interruptions)—and as I sit here on 1 April, I have completed the appliqué. Believe me, my shoulders and neck are telling me so!

I did encounter a few problems, though; I had backed the pomegranates with an iron-on non-woven interfacing to give me slightly more bulk for appliquéing—it gives a better stitch and prevents the appliqué stitching from drawing the fabric in and changing the size of the panel.

However, the non-woven interfacing actually made the appliquéing more difficult, as it felted with use and prevented my being able to get a smooth outline. Also, the 60/8 needles kept breaking the thread. I changed to a larger needle, a Metafil 80/10, which has a larger eye, and achieved success.

A section of the first lower appliquéd border features simple shapes like this folk-art star. It contains completely different motifs from the corresponding border at the top.

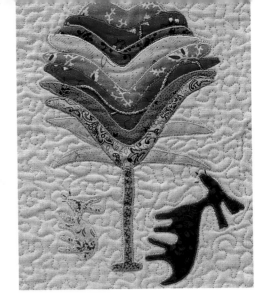

There are 250 individual pieces in the wide cream borders. Even such naïve shapes as the deer required embellishment.

Even though I cut the fabric larger, I have a discrepancy of about ½," so I am now going to have to be a little more creative.

A grand total 318 individual pieces are involved in the first appliqué border. No wonder it took so long! I look longingly at the rest of the borders. How I wish I were a little further advanced—it is really hard, physically, to do this amount of intense work. On the other hand, the enjoyment I get from looking at the quilt is immense, and I know that pleasure will last me a lifetime.

Okay . . . completed . . . the first round of appliquéd borders.

WEDNESDAY, 3 APRIL, 2002

Late last night (against my better judgment), I sewed my finished appliqué border to the existing quilt. Only to find that it wasn't going to fit with the pieced border! Eek! I was so tired, having been in the shed since 4:00 a.m. Maybe there was even a degree of desperation.

However, this morning the brain works better, and I am able to make better judgments. I adjusted the border by adding a little extra at both the top and bottom—creative license. I find, in looking at the photos of the original quilt, that the makers used creative license in this very same border, but their license took a different form.

Next, a pair of vertical borders made of the larger Elies blocks, then everything else is appliqué.

Hard Work and Deadlines

FRIDAY, 5 APRIL, 2002

I spent two days completing the illustrations for the strips in the next full border, using the photos I took at the museum in Bautzen. My method of working is that I first isolate individual figures, then make pen sketches of each to use for appliqué templates. It takes a lot of time, but I must admit it is quite relaxing, compared to appliquéing.

These two vertical strips are quite symmetrical, with some figures appearing just once, some four times. I needed to reverse some of the illustrations, which I did by putting them through the scanner, then turning them over and re-scanning. There are 250 individual pieces on the two vertical borders, which are alike. The horizontal borders are alike, although different from the vertical borders.

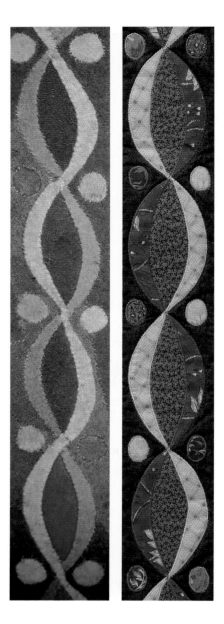

The oval appliqué shape became known as a *pomegranate*. A chain of these ovals takes on the appearance of twining ribbons.

WEDNESDAY, APRIL 17, 2002

Well, I have completed part of the vertical border. It was hard work, but I am really pleased with the results.

Yesterday I spent completely on fitting the borders to the quilt. I had great difficulty. I wasn't satisfied with the last pieced border, that last row of ten Elies blocks—the proportion just didn't seem right to me.

So I took the borders off again, and, using EQ4, I decided to cut the Elies blocks smaller. I did have the two extra blocks, so with the calculations from the computer, I figured to trim the blocks from 7" down to 5¾." I also added one more block to each side. The border now fits perfectly, and I think the proportion is much better.

Even though it took an entire day, it was worth it. I think these narrower borders are going to give me an additional 2" to play with when I sew the final borders onto the quilt.

I spent an hour or so with my friend Vera Lloyd this morning, assisting her with a project she's working on for the Houston show, then we went out to lunch. I didn't realize how much I would enjoy being away from the restrictions of the shed. I love working on the quilt, but it is all-encompassing. Pauline came back for tea, then we worked on her Houston project again. At the same time, I prepared the appliqué figures for the next border. I believe that I need to appliqué at least four images a day if I am going to complete the quilt on time. Plus, I will also need to prepare the shapes for the next day's appliqués.

THURSDAY, 18 APRIL, 2002

I worked hard today, and I am paying for it physically—my back and shoulders suffer. I try to be sensible and vary my work to allow me time away from the machine. In fact, I began appliquéing at 7:00 this morning and finished at 7:30 this evening, then prepared the appliqué shapes for tomorrow, did a small amount of embroidery on the quilt, and wrote up this précis. Finally, at 9:30 p.m., I can go inside and read before bed.

SUNDAY, 21 APRIL, 2002

I was only able to work on the quilt for half a day on Friday. I had to attend to some much-needed shopping. It's such a nuisance having to purchase food! Son Jinda came with me and, after popping down to K-Mart, he attended to one of his school assignments by looking at an exhibition in the art gallery. Then we went to the market for tea.

After making it home with all the shopping, I had a rare couple of hours to myself while the family went to the basketball finals. So I managed another couple of hours' worth of appliquéing before bed.

Saturday was a bit of a loss as I spent most of the day on the computer, and a brief respite in the form of visitors also held me up. But today I have completed two-thirds of the second appliqué border.

TUESDAY, 23 APRIL, 2002

As I work on the quilt, I give way to thoughts that go back to 1776. I'd love to know who designed the quilt—was it a soldier, far from his family and loved ones? Did working on the quilt give him some comfort? How many uniforms went into making the quilt? Close inspection shows that the background was pieced and patched in almost every block and border. Were the uniforms old ones, or could they be the uniforms of comrades who died? Where did the needles and thread come from? Did they go to war toting needle and thread? Did they sit around the camp fire each night and work on the quilt as a group, or did one driven individual make it?

MONDAY, 29 APRIL, 2002

Almost a week since I have written. Finally, the second appliqué border is completed and on the quilt. Now I need to place the sashing around the appliqué border and then I can get on with the illustrations for the third appliqué border. There is still a degree of urgency, and my heart thumps at the thought of just what I have to complete.

Within two months of resuming work on the quilt, I had the first appliqué border ready. The two vertical "pomegranate" borders (shown in progress) are identical; the two horizontal borders (seen at extreme right) are different. It was important to me that the tips of the pomegranate shapes align with the seams that joined the Hourglass blocks.

I wonder if I am alienating myself from some of my friends, as I have not seen some of them for quite a while. But, on the other hand, I do hope they understand that I am working hard on this project, and if they are really my friends, they will contact me.

It was cold out here this morning, just 6°C (about 42°F). I feel like such a dog in this old tracksuit, but it's warm; I always have the company of the real dogs—Turbo, Ralf, and Buddy.

SATURDAY, 11 MAY, 2002

Goodness! It's been twelve days since I entered any information into this book, but, believe me, I've worked really hard. I feel a bit of a failure if I don't write the information down, but it gets in my way sometimes.

I have now completed all of the illustrations for the entire quilt. Those for the third border alone took a total of eight hours.

Battling with Hundreds of Appliqués

MONDAY, 13 MAY, 2002

Now, I must tackle the large black borders for the top and bottom of the quilt. They consist of sixteen soldiers on foot, four naïve birds in the trees, two central crests and the date, and eight soldiers on horses.

TUESDAY, 14 MAY, 2002

It has taken two days to prepare eight horses for appliqué. There are 120 individual pieces.

FRIDAY, 19 MAY, 2002

Whew! I spent the entire day—6:00 a.m. until now, 9:51 p.m.—machine-embroidering with a twisted gold thread, difficult to handle. Although I changed the needle to one with a wider hole, the thread still strips back. I finally decided to drop the feed dogs in order to accommodate this tiresome thread and appliquéd freehand, except that I stitched the swords in the normal manner, with the feed dogs up.

The light-background (second appliqué) borders are quite symmetrical, although the vertical strips are different from the horizontals. This detail is shown in side-by-side comparison of old and new.

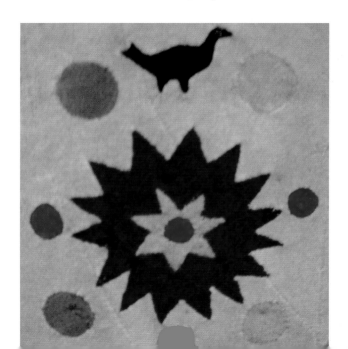

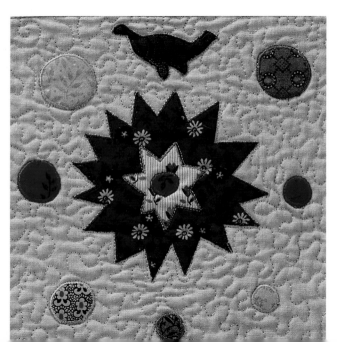

The soldiers' uniforms were enlivened by the addition of gold machine embroidery; I experimented until I found a nifty way of preventing the gold thread from stripping back. These photos from the new quilt show the soldiers with and without gold embellishments

Finally I have finished for the day, and my eyes are drooping. Eight soldiers now have all their finery: it takes an hour for each one. The gold embroidery makes a huge difference in the look of the appliqué.

MONDAY, 27 MAY, 2002

I have been working really hard on the appliqué soldiers, and finally, last night, 26 May, I finished this border. It feels like I've climbed Mt. Everest. The horses are really interesting. For some reason, there is one white horse at the top left-hand side, but all the others are blue.

The gold embroidery was another thing. It took one hour each to embroider the soldiers and horses. The jolly thread kept breaking. I used every method I knew to get it to run smoothly through the machine. Finally, after many frustrating hours, I came up with a novel idea, and it seems to work. I took a piece of ⅛" cord about 8" long and soaked it in virgin olive oil (I didn't have any machine oil). I then wiped the cord through the thread holder of the machine, and voilà, it worked like a treat! The gold thread fed smoothly, at least for a short time.

It took considerable time to correctly cut the background strips for the soldier borders. I decided to make them wider than necessary and trim them to the correct size after they had been appliquéd. Then I sewed them to the bottom and top of the quilt. IT LOOKS GREAT!

This has been my favorite part of the quilt.

Now I must set myself a schedule to complete the final border.

Chapter 5

The Final Push

*The borders go on, the quilting begins,
and friends far and wide rally
around for the final stitches*

Flurries and Frustrations

As the borders nearing completion at last, you can imagine my mounting excitement as the full surface of *1776* came together before my eyes. Of course, I discovered that the larger the quilt grew, the trickier my job became. Those endless borders! Some are so narrow my fingers felt clumsy as I strived to cut impossibly long and slender strips of fabric and feed them through my machine. Remember, too, that I was still balancing a frantic work schedule and an always hectic home life during the long sleepless nights I stayed up with *1776*, I learned the true meaning of the word *obsession*.

TUESDAY, 28 MAY, 2002

Today I'm finishing the sashing that frames the final appliqué border; although there are three colors in the sashing on the original quilt, I will only use two. For this border, I need to cut 2"-wide strips that will be cut back to 1½". If I cut the strips wider than needed, it is easier to get a perfect fit and edge. My rule is: cut oversize to begin with, then trim back.

Frustration! It has taken an entire day to complete the sashing, and, for Pete's sake, it's just a 1½" border. After unpicking it several times I think I finally have it correct. Adding a narrow strip to a very large quilt is difficult to do, because I have to be absolutely accurate, and fitting the quilt, which is quite large at its present stage, under the machine needle gives me a headache.

Tuesday, 11 June, 2002

The past two weeks have been a flurry of work, and I'm very happy with the results. However, the quilt is ever present, and the work is pressing. I had to quilt a sample and finish off a quilt for the Houston exhibition. With teaching and extra-curricular activities, I value the time I can spare in the shed, but I'm putting in some fifteen-hour days.

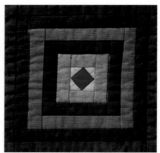

In the next-to-last appliquéd border, new shapes appear. I gave the geometric ones names appropriate to the history of the quilt. TOP: I named this modified bulls-eye design the "Sorbian" block. BOTTOM: I named this square-within-a square, the "Wendish" block.

This one I named the "Bautzen" block.

The next-to-last appliquéd border has some 50-plus blocks. I have completed 36 and am about to put together the next eight. Even though I'm ready to go, since I have already drawn, scanned, and reversed the patterns for these border blocks, I can't help but think that I could have made another small quilt with the 54 blocks required for this border.

The quilt is growing in size with each border I complete. Even though I have the design on the computer, it sure is a shock when I see the actual quilt taking shape. Yes, it's REALLY big.

Appliqué, appliqué, appliqué . . . cooking, shopping, and cleaning take a back seat. Maybe it's lucky that the builders have come in and I have another legitimate excuse not to clean the house!

Tuesday, 2 July, 2002

Not only did the shopping, cleaning, and cooking take a back seat, I have found little time to document my work in the past three weeks, due to its intensity.

The next-to-last appliquéd border contained, in addition to sixteen soldiers and four of Germany's double-headed eagle, interesting vignettes of tightrope walkers, men smoking long pipes, several abstract shapes, and a virtual arboretum of plants. A block containing two birds, one of them a stork with a baby-shaped bundle in his beak, was used at each of the four corners.

SUNDAY, 7 JULY, 2002

Oh goodness, time is weighing hard on my hands. It's Sunday and I have to finish these borders. I don't think I can do it. I think I have to omit the final appliqué border of pomegranates. I have promised myself to have the quilt finished by 31 December, 2002. I know how long it will take me to quilt it, and I want to make the deadline to enter it into the exhibition in Houston.

Help Is at Hand and the End Is in Sight

TUESDAY, 9 JULY, 2002

Hearing of my plight, my friends arrived last night with dinner, candy, a bottle of wine, and lots of encouragement. They ironed my stash, tidied my fabric, and gave me lots of much-needed support.

I used Cherrywood fabric for the final appliqué border, although it's not the same as the original quilt. I pieced the border background strips together and prepared the appliqué—100 pomegranates and 200 one-inch circles.

TUESDAY, 16 JULY, 2002

It took an entire week to appliqué the final border sections, and I am grateful that my buddies gave me the encouragement to finish. After so much work, I am anxious for the quilt top to be absolutely completed.

I'm finally stitching the borders on, after finishing the appliquéing. The appliqué circles were really hard to get accurate and neat, as they seemed to multiply and they were so boring, but I couldn't let the standard slip.

I begin to despair. Last night I worked so long, I fell asleep at the machine.

WEDNESDAY, 24 JULY, 2002

Tomorrow is another milestone. The quilt will be sandwiched, and I am anxious to begin to quilt it. I keep wondering how heavy it's going to be. I have machine-quilted three quilts this size before, and I know that at first it is difficult. But it's just a technique, and, as I have all the advantages of a great sewing table, machine, and chair, I think I'll do it well.

However, as I'm preparing to put on the final border, I keep seeing mistakes in my work. Boy, I can see heaps of mistakes—thread showing through, a couple of missed stitches! Am I paranoid? In the scheme of things, do a few stitches matter? Yes, they do.

A review of the entire quilt top was necessary; I made the required corrections.

Now for the very last, the turkey red border. I've had to search high and low for the fabric for this part of the quilt. I actually purchased it from five different sources. The color varies a little, but I don't think it matters too much. I am coming to the end, and in a way I'm a bit sad. I have to teach for the next week so no work will be done on the quilt.

THURSDAY, 1 AUGUST, 2002

Finally, I have completed the border and the top is now complete. I showed it for the first time to a group of people with whom I was teaching. It was interesting to gauge their comments. One comment from a fellow teacher at that venue was, "I don't think it will go well in competition, because it's a copy."

ABOVE: The final borders are ready to be stitched to the quilt. During the appliquéing of the circles, I began to fantasize that they were multiplying and I'd never finish sewing them on. LEFT: The one hundred pomegranates of the final border were made in 52 different color schemes.

However, I was surprised at the reaction of my fellow quilters. Everyone loved the quilt, and I began to understand that it was special. When you put so much of yourself into the quilt, it's difficult to know just how good it is. I didn't make it for competition; I made it for myself. However, now I want to share it with the world, and I'm afraid that if one person sees it as a copy, maybe that's the way everyone will see it. Well heck! I just don't care.

Quilting 1776

It was cold and almost the middle of winter. The builders had moved in; we were having the entire bottom floor of the house treated for salt damp. That meant that all my furniture was out under the veranda at the back, installed under blue tarps. It was freezing cold. Keith slept on the floor in the living room upstairs, and I had the small room. It was far more pleasant in the shed. This was when I machine-quilted *1776*.

I didn't keep a journal during the quilting. It was rather boring. I just wanted to get on and get it finished, and sitting at the computer was not in the equation. I worked day and night for several weeks, and often the days blended into one another. I learned the meaning of obsession in a very personal way. When I realized that I was going to make the deadline I gave myself to finish—Christmas 2002—I began to relax a little. I had a visitor from the United States, and took three weeks off to tour with her. I had quite a few teaching commitments as well, but by Christmas 2002 I had the quilt completed with the binding on.

I don't know the exact date that I decided the quilt was *completely* finished; I played with it many times, going back and back again, quilting more and more. I put the last quilting stitches in one day in May 2003. The next month the quilt traveled with me to the United States.

Here my journal ends. The rest of this chapter describes how I executed the quilting of *1776*.

Making the Quilt "Sandwich"

Thank goodness I had machine-quilted three large pieces prior to *1776*, because experience had taught me to use a walking foot and to begin by stitching along the straight lines of the quilt. In this series of three photos, I gradually disappear behind a growing mountain of quilt top!

First, I assembled the backing from the larger pieces of fabric—I love pieced backings. Finally it was big enough—3" larger all around than the quilt top—and ready to go.

With the backing fabric right side down on my big six-foot by eight-foot table, I clamped it securely to the edges of the table, stretching it taut. I'm very fussy at this stage. It is really important to get the fabric pulled as straight and tight as you possibly can. (Tip: If the quilt is not so large as *1776*, and does not reach to the edge of the table, which it must do if you are going to clamp it, you can tape the backing securely to the table with a firm, wide masking tape.)

I then spread the batting, cut to the same size as the backing, over the wrong side of the backing. My batting, Warm and Natural®, was wide enough, thankfully, that I didn't have to seam it. I gently spread and smoothed the batting over the backing until I was satisfied that all the bumps were out. Batting has a tendency to stick to the fabric beneath it, which was a help in getting it perfectly flat.

Finally, I lay the quilt top, wrong side down, on the batting and repeated the spreading and smoothing process. When I was satisfied that the top was correctly positioned on the batting and backing and was completely flat, I clamped all three layers firmly to the table. Then I basted the quilt—every inch. I used a bright thread, began in the center, and used a circular pat-

News of the Quilt Begins to Get Out

After a great deal of consideration I decided, in early Spring 2002, to let people outside a small circle of friends and family know about my quilt. A small notice that I was reproducing a German quilt made by soldiers in 1776 was published in the May 2002 edition of the *Quilters Companion* (an Australian publication now distributed in the United States and Great Britain). I began to feel very silly when people asked me just what the quilt was. So I threw caution to the wind and published a few photos on my Web page. I'm pleased I did, because it created a great deal of interest. Here are just a few of the comments I received.

"Pam, I hope you are going to write a pattern booklet of the 1776 quilt. I would be interested in purchasing one if you do." *Dale Anne in central Saskatchewan*

"I think your soldiers' quilt could become as important as the "Dear Jane" quilt. Thank you for sharing it with us." *Diana*

"Your reproduction quilt is stunning! Thanks for sharing it with the British Quilt History Group. I hope you will be entering it in some American shows and/or doing an article on it for *Quilter's Newsletter Magazine*. Beautiful job. It's a great quilt too." *Kimberly Wulfert, California*

"I love the quilt! I particularly love the naive borders. How did you come to find the quilt and why [did you] reproduce it?

You have taken on an enormous project and have done a wonderful job." *Nicole Hester Revesby, New South Wales*

"That quilt is one of the most wonderful things I have ever seen. Pam, you are creating such a masterpiece, and the fact that there is a family connection to that town in Germany just gives me goose bumps. You WERE meant to do that quilt. And we are so lucky to be able to see it on your Web site." *Betsy, Montana*

Another woman contacted me wanting information on the quilt; she came from Silesia as a child, not far from Bautzen, and was interested in the *Quilters Companion* article. I sent her two photos—one of the original quilt, another of part of my reproduction. When the two were side by side, I realized how accurately I had re-constructed the quilt.

I was sometimes bewildered by the insistence of some viewers that my quilt was "just a copy." That tired me out more than the sewing!

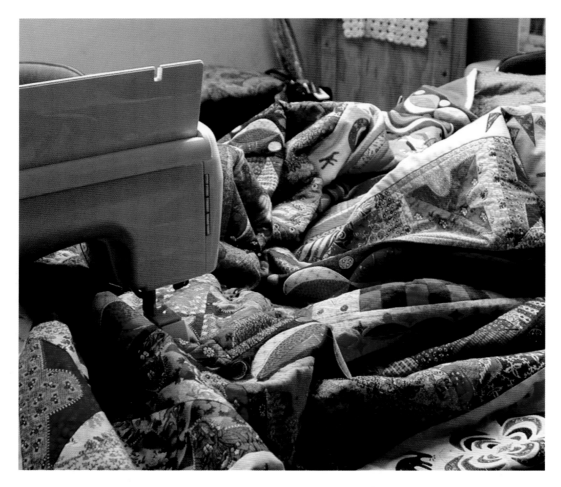

tern to hold the three layers together. (Tip: Sometimes I baste in a 2" square grid. On smaller pieces, rather than basting with thread, I will often pin-baste at 3"-square intervals, using special rust-proof safety pins for quilters.)

MACHINE QUILTING

How do you fit a nine-foot by ten-foot quilt under a normal machine? "Scrunch" is the word. As long as the quilt is thoroughly basted, you can push and pull as much as you need, and believe me, at times I sure needed to do a lot of pushing and pulling. I didn't roll the quilt, or put it over my shoulder (as some quilters recommend), because it's too darned heavy; I just scrunched, and created a well in the middle to sew on.

In order to meet the physical challenge of handling such a weighty piece, I raised myself above the level of the quilt so that I didn't have to lift it. I did that by lowering my sewing table (three draftsman's tables pushed together, actually) and by raising my sewing chair so that I sat some 20" above the machine. In fact, the chair was so high that I could barely reach the foot pedal. However, that left my arms free to steer and manipulate the quilt as necessary.

Once I was set up, I checked to make sure that I had excellent lighting, the importance of which I cannot over-emphasize. My Ott light gives me superior visibility, ensuring a good color match between thread and fabric, and making it possible for me to place my stitches exactly where I want them.

I used a rayon thread color-matched to the fabric exactly; needless to say, I had to change the thread frequently. I matched the bobbin thread color to the quilt backing, which was red. I chose, as always, my favorite needle for quilting: the very slender 60/8 sharp. I must confess that it takes a little practice to use such fine needles without frequently breaking them. If you break such needles consistently, the reason could be that you are forcing or pulling the quilt, rather than letting it flow on its own through the machine. However, if the fine needle proves to be just too difficult, you could use a 70/10 sharp or a quilting needle.

I change my needle each day of quilting. Sometimes, when I am appliquéing, I change the needle twice a day. It has proven to work for me in giving the even stitching I demand.

The quilting thread matches the appliqué thread wherever possible. Look carefully at the stems to see the "appliqué ditching stitch," my name for the straight-stitch line of quilting placed as near as possible the appliqué stitching. The term for this technique is called "stitching-in-the-ditch" on patchwork seams, thus my name adaptation for appliqué seams. Although the stippling stitches are barely visible, because the thread is so closely matched to the fabric, they add texture to the background.

QUILTING SEQUENCE

Here is the sequence I followed and the stitches I used in machine-quilting *1776*.

1. Taking that first stitch on my trusty Janome 9000 was nerve-wracking. I decided to begin by quilting the "frame" of the quilt—that is, every straight line in the quilt where a walking foot could be used. The walking foot is an ingenious invention and absolutely essential for machine quilting. Its dual feed extension ensures that the three layers of the quilt feed evenly through the machine. I began in the center and worked out to the edge of the quilt, using a 1.8 stitch length, the same length I use for freehand quilting, on every straight line in the quilt.

2. In the center block, I freehand-quilted around each of the appliqué images with a thread that matched the appliqué. In fact, it was the exact same thread I appliquéd with. The stitch is almost like a stitch in the ditch, because it goes right next to the edge of the appliqué stitch. I call this an "appliqué ditching stitch." Although some authorities suggest dropping the machine's feed dog when doing free-hand quilting, I never do that. I find that I have much more control over my machine with the feed dogs up in place.

3. With the exception of the star, the rest of the block was stippled every ¼" with thread that matched the background fabric. Stippling is basically free-hand quilting, used to fill in the background. I always draw my stippling pattern out on a piece of paper, over and over, until it is programmed into my brain. Then when I start stitching, it just seems to flow. I sew at about the same pace as I draw, slowly and deliberately. I am of a different school from those quilting teachers who advise their students to put on some lively music, relax, and just sew fast and furiously when stippling, letting the random pattern unfold beneath their needle. That doesn't work for me.

4. All of the Elies blocks were stitched with an "appliqué ditching stitch" right next to the blanket stitching. I used the same gold rayon thread as in the appliqué stitching.

5. The checkerboard blocks were stitched in the ditch on the straight lines—that is, around every check. I used a smoke-colored monofilament thread. I "appliqué ditch-stitched" the appliqués of the narrow borders, then stippled the background of the borders with thread that matched the fabric.

6. All of the appliquéd borders were quilted in the same manner—"appliqué ditch-stitched" around the appliqué and stippling in the background.

7. In the final pomegranate border, I "appliqué ditch-stitched" the images, but I stippled only in the center of the pomegranates.

8. The final, plain turkey red border was quilted in straight lines placed ¼" apart.

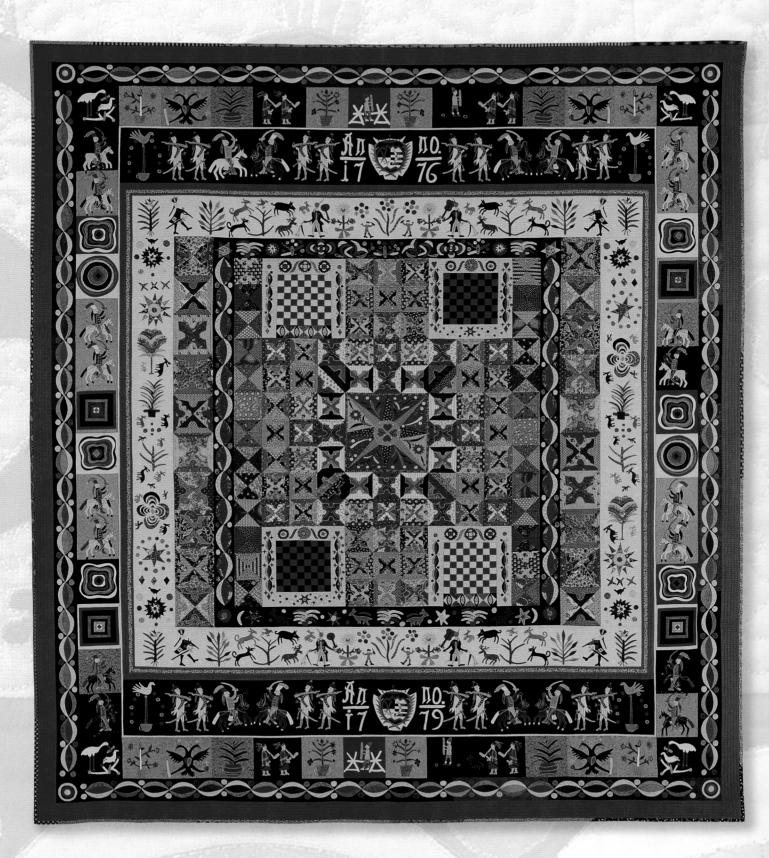

PART TWO

RECREATING

1776

Section by Section

Chapter 6

Building Out from the Center Square

I describe and provide step-by-step directions for making the center portion of 1776

When most people look at *1776*, they see it as an appliqué quilt. However, there is a fair amount of traditional piecing involved in making my version. In fact, the very first task—making the center square—is a small piecing project. Look carefully and you will see that the square consists of a simple *Mariner's Compass*, with four long compass points and four shorter ones. The square is filled out by eight large triangles. Rather than piece the center circle, I simply fused my fabric circle over the raw edges of all those compass points and finished it with machine embroidery--what an easy way to tidy things up! The flowers and leaves that embellish the large triangles, are, of course, appliqué.

1776 is basically a central medallion quilt, one in which a distinctive center block is surrounded by numerous borders. In classic central medallion quilts, the center block is not repeated, although border designs may be, and usually are, used more than once. Additionally, the borders are made with a number of different needlework techniques, including patchwork, appliqué, embroidery and/or quilting. Although *1776* shares all these characteristics, it also presents a slight deviation from traditional medallion quilts, apparent in the manner in which the four checkerboard blocks are used. In a strictly typical medallion-style quilt, the checkerboards should function as cornerstones in an elaborate border. However, in *1776*, they are independent motifs that could be said to enlarge the medallion from the relatively small star-

like block in the exact center of the quilt to the rectangle described by their outer perimeters. This is only one of the fascinating aspects of the quilt—there are many, and that is why the quilt so easily captured and held my interest for the years it took to make it.

As I worked through my photographs of the original quilt, I discovered that the quilt is comprised of as many as twenty different sections. The sections are repeated as needed to fill out the design. Some sections are used twice, some four times. In one round of borders, for example, the side borders are identical, but the top and bottom borders are different, not only from the side borders, but from one another. To my way of counting, there were three different sections involved in that one border round.

The sections are composed mainly of blocks, either patchwork or appliqué. (However, six of the border sections are made of strips of fabric, rather than blocks, onto which appliquéd figures were worked.) Another of the great joys of deciphering *1776* was the discovery of two patchwork blocks never seen before. I named one after my grandfather Elies and the other I just called the Notch block. I also had great satisfaction in naming some of the appliqué blocks to reflect the heritage of the quilt.

In this chapter and the one that follows, I offer directions and patterns for making each section, in order that you can have access to the entire quilt. Although I will be surprised if many of you decide to reproduce the whole quilt, I hope you will find the images so compelling that you will want to use some of them in your own smaller projects, as several of my friends in Australia have done. We call them "offspring!"(See Part Three.)

Center Square

Although I rarely make blocks from templates, I have found this way of piecing to be the most accurate by far of all the many different techniques I tried as I labored over this block. I machine-stitched the pieces together.

Step 4

MATERIALS

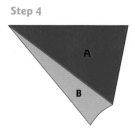

Large background triangles: four fat quarters of fabric, each in a different color

Star points: one fat quarter each for long points and short points (contrast colors)

Center circle: scrap of fabric in desired color

Hearts: scraps of fabric in two different colors

Leafy appliqué and small appliqué circles: scraps of fabric in desired colors

Narrow border around perimeter of block: ¼ yard of fabric in desired color

Fusible web, stabilizer, and template plastic

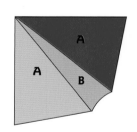

MAKING THE CENTER SQUARE (MAKE 1)

See templates A to E and template sets F to H on pages 136 to 137.

1. Make templates by tracing pattern pieces A, B, C, D, and E onto template plastic. Mark the grainline on each template. Use a tiny (⅟₁₆") hole punch to make a hole at each angle on A, B, and C, exactly where the seamlines cross. This will facilitate matching pieces to one another.

2. Place template A on the right side of one fat quarter of fabric; trace the shape two times. Using a mechanical pencil, mark the point where the seamlines cross through the hole you made in the template. Repeat on the other three fat quarters until all eight pieces have been traced. Note that the template must be reversed for half the pieces. In the same way, trace template B four times each, and template D once, each on its corresponding fabric. Use template C to cut four circles and template E to cut four heart shapes from fabric.

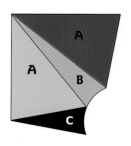

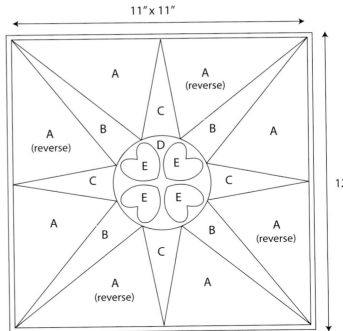

11" x 11"

12" x 12"

Step 5

Step 6

3. Carefully cut out each pattern piece. From the border fabric, cut two strips measuring ¾" x 11½" and two strips measuring ¾" x 12". From the stabilizer, cut a 15" square.

4. Lay out the pieces in the order in which they will be sewn together. Sew the long diagonal of an A piece to either side of each long star point B. Make four. Sew a star point C to each to complete a corner unit. Sew the four corner units together. Add stablizer to the wrong side of the pieced block.

5. Following the directions on pages 62 to 63, prepare, then fuse center circle template D in place. Note that the circle will hide the raw edges of the shapes pieced so far. In the same way, attach heart shapes E. Following the directions on page 67, machine embroider around the circle and the hearts.

6. Again following the directions on pages 62 to 63 and page 67, prepare, fuse, then machine embroider each motif in template sets F (flower), G (leaves 1), and H (leaves 2). Note that you will need to reverse G to create two mirror-image versions. Use the photograph as a guide to placing the motifs on each A fabric.

7. Press the block and trim it to 11½" square. Sew the short strips from step 3 on the top and bottom of the block, then sew the longer strips onto the sides. Press again, then check that the block, with its borders, accurately measures 12" square (include outer seam allowance). Trim to size if necessary.

Machine Appliqué

Accuracy must be maintained throughout every step of making an appliqué motif. Each section, every detail, of the motif will be drawn onto fusing web; those sections and details will be cut out, and they must all fit perfectly into a completed motif. This is no time to get into a rush. As I have said before, I find I actually work faster by going slowly and carefully, because I make fewer time-consuming mistakes. Also, since this is raw-edge appliqué, which eliminates the necessity of turning under a seam allowance, the work goes much faster than with traditional hand appliqué.

Prepare Motifs

1. Draw each image for the appliqué motif onto the paper side of fusible web by placing the web over the pattern and tracing. I find that a mechanical pencil keeps a sharp point, as opposed to wooden pencils with softer leads. (This is when the reverse

pattern comes into play, especially if the motif is a directional one. The image you trace onto the fusible web must be the mirror image of the motif, since it will be applied to the back of the appliqué fabric. If you don't use the reversed image, all your finished motifs will be going in the wrong direction.)

2. Cut the shapes out of the fusible web/paper, leaving a margin of at least ¼". You do not have to worry excessively about accurate cutting at this point; basically, you are simply separating the shapes from one another.

3. Choosing the ideal fabric for each appliqué motif is one of the most creative and enjoyable parts of this process. Once you are satisfied with your choice, cut a piece from the fabric about

the same size as its corresponding fusible web shape—again, accuracy is not an issue at this point.

4. Following the instructions that come with the product, iron the fusible web to the wrong side of the fabric. Make sure the glue side is down on the fabric and the paper side is up. Leave the paper in place to use as a guide for cutting and placing.

5. Cut out each shape—this point is often very fiddly, because you must use a smooth stroke and maintain accuracy, cutting exactly on the drawn line. Because this is raw-edge appliqué, a smooth edge makes the finished piece look as good as possible. It is important to be very organized. I usually put the cut pieces in individual re-sealable bags, or store them in a plastic file in a sequence that is easy to handle.

6. Next comes the assembly of the appliqués, most of which consist of multiple pieces. Use a transparent heatproof

so, the paper just slipped off, saving lots of time—and my nails as well.)

Fuse Motifs

7. The next step is the positioning of the assembled appliqué shapes onto their backgrounds, whether border strips or blocks. Although it was extra work, I drew the outlines of the appliqué shapes onto the background border strips and blocks. It gave me an accurate and invaluable guide for final positioning of those shapes. In order to avoid excess handling of the appliqués, I worked with only one shape at a time, placing and stitching it in place before going to the next one. To fuse, press each piece of each motif firmly in place. (See also the manufacturer's directions for using fusible web.) Machine embroider around each motif, as explained on page 67.

craft sheet or mat and build each shape separately (See photo on page 22). Place the drawn pattern under the craft mat and follow it for accurate placement of

all the images are correct—for example, all horses and soldiers are the same dimensions and fit within the background properly. It is only when the entire motif is complete that I remove the paper from the fusible web. (Tip: I found that I was ruining my fingernails when I separated the paper from the fabric. I don't have fancy nails, but they had been splitting, and I suddenly realized how much damage I was doing with this jolly appliqué. Dang. Hmmm. I also noticed that if I separated the paper from the fabric immediately after ironing it on, it was really difficult. However, if I prepared the pieces, then waited an hour or

8. Once the border or block is assembled, I back it with a stabilizer fabric such as Quilt Light.® Other suitable stabilizers are voile and similar lightweight fabrics. The stabilizer prevents the border from stretching as it is machine-stitched in position on the quilt.

the pieces. At this point, I always think carefully about which piece needs to go down first, second, third, and so on. I then iron each piece on individually.

Assemble the entire appliqué in this manner. It is a very efficient way to work, because where the surface of the craft mat meets the appliqué piece, the glue remains on the fabric. However, where fabric is adhered to fabric, it is there to stay. This method ensures that

First Pieced Border

This border consists of twelve small Elies blocks and four Notch blocks. Notice that there are two sizes of Elies blocks in 1776; the smaller one is used here in the center of the quilt, and the larger one is used to make the two vertical panels that bound the larger center section of the quilt (see page 59).

The Notch block, an interesting and unique pattern, is repeated only four times on this entire quilt, yet it has many possibilities for use in your other patchwork quilts. Because four fabrics are used in each block, it is an easy way to add lots of color to a project.

MATERIALS

ELIES BLOCK

Two-color background triangles: twelve 6" squares of contrasting fabrics (for example, half light and half dark).

Two-color center motif: twelve 4½" squares of contrasting fabrics

Fusible web

NOTCH BLOCK

Two-color background: four 5½" squares of contrasting fabrics

Two-color center motif: four 6" x 3" rectangles of contrasting fabrics

Fusible web

MAKING ELIES BLOCK (MAKE 12 SMALL BLOCKS)

See template A (small Elies block) on page 138.

Step 1

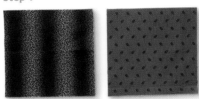

1. For each block, cut two 6" squares from two contrasting fabrics and two 4½" squares from two different contrasting fabrics. Place two contrasting-color 6" squares right sides together, aligning the outer edges.

2. Place a ruler diagonally across them from corner to corner, and draw a line exactly through the diagonal center. Sew ¼" either side of the diagonal line. Press to set the stitching.

Step 2

3. Cut the block in half on the drawn line. Open up each half to reveal two half-square triangles sewn together down the center; press the seam allowances to the darker triangle. Open out. You will now have a pair of identical half-square triangle blocks.

4. Right sides together, place the two blocks together, matching a light triangle to a dark one, and setting the seams next to one another. You can do this by pushing the seams together with your fingers until you feel them "lock" into place. Pin along the seamline securely so the block doesn't move.

Step 3

5. Place a ruler diagonally across the block from corner to corner, in the opposite direction from the seam, and draw a line exactly through the diagonal center of the block. Cut the block in half on the drawn line. Open out each half to reveal two identical 5½" Hourglass squares. Press the center seam allowances open.

Steps 4 and 5

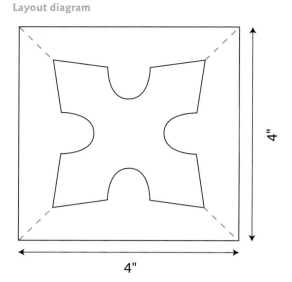

4"

4"

Step 6

Step 7

Step 9

Step 10

6. Repeat Steps 2 through 5 with the 4 ½" squares. To make each Elies block, you will now have one large and one small Hourglass block.

7. Trace template A for the center four-petaled shape from page 138 onto the paper side of the fusible web. (Be certain to use the pattern for the small Elies block.) Iron the fusible web to the back of a small 4 ½" Hourglass square.

8. Cut out the four-petal shape with scissors, making the edges as smooth as possible. Do not remove the paper.

9. Pair up the four-petal shape with the large Hourglass square. Remove the paper from the back of the four-petal shape and carefully place it on the Hourglass unit, matching diagonal seamline to diagonal seamline. Using fusible web and following the manufacturer's directions, fuse the center to the background. (Tip: If you make all the Hourglass units at once, then all the center four-petal shapes, you can experiment with placing different centers on different backgrounds until you are satisfied with your fabric combinations.)

10. Following the directions for machine embroidery on page 67, stitch around the edges of the center shape. Test the stitch to get it to about ⅛" wide. I used a gold-colored rayon thread for the top and also for the bobbin. When the embroidery is complete, turn the block to the wrong side and trim away the portion of the background underneath the center shape, using a small, sharp scissors. You can forego this step, but the block will be rather bulky. Carefully trim the blocks to 4 ½" (which includes the outer seam allowance).

Machine Embroidery

The method I use to sew my appliqué motifs to their respective backgrounds is basically a form of machine embroidery that utilizes a zig-zag or blanket stitch. Choose a thread color that matches the fabric of the appliqué as closely as possible. This may require changing colors several times within one motif. Use the same thread in the bobbin as in the upper threading of the machine.

An open-toed presser foot enables you to clearly see the cut edge of the appliqué, and I highly recommend that you get one for your machine if you do a lot of this work. However, an ordinary plastic, see-through, foot can be used successfully.

1. Set the machine to a zig-zag or blanket stitch, adjusting the stitch length and width to suit your personal preference. I prefer a 1.5 stitch width and a .35 stitch length. It is a good idea to sew a few test lines until you are pleased with the appearance of the stitch.

2. Adjust the bobbin tension by manipulating the tension dial on the top of your sewing machine. I like to take it down to about 3, because a rounded look is given

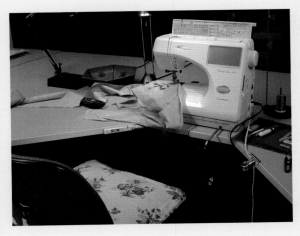

to the appliqué stitch when the bobbin thread is tightened and pulls the upper thread down into the fabric.

3. Position the needle at the beginning of the stitching and secure the thread ends by reducing the stitch length to zero and stitching in place several times. If you wish, you can ensure that the back of your work is as clean as the front by bringing the end of the bobbin thread to the surface as you start stitching. Take a couple of stitches, then lift the end of the upper thread to tease the loop of the bobbin thread to the surface. Use a pin to tug on the loop until the bobbin thread end comes all the way up to the surface of the quilt. Hold both thread ends as you stitch in place three or four times.

4. Sew around the shape smoothly and evenly, keeping the edge of the appliqué piece in the center of the stitch.

5. Secure the end of the stitching in one of two ways: reduce the stitch length to zero and take several stitches in the same place, or manually pull the threads to the back side of the quilt, tie them in a square knot, then weave the thread ends into the body of the stitching by threading them through a hand needle.

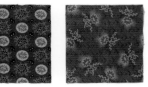

MAKING NOTCH BLOCK (MAKE 4)

See template A (Notch block) on page 139.

1. For each block, cut two 5½" squares from contrasting fabric.

2. Place the two 5½" squares right sides together, aligning the outer edges. Follow steps 2 to 3 for making the Elies block on page 65. You will now have a pair of identical half-square triangle blocks, but you will use only one for each Notch block.

3. For each block, cut two 6" x 3" rectangles from contrasting fabrics. Right sides together and outer edges aligned, stitch the pair of rectangles together along one long side. Press the seam allowances open.

4. Trace the pattern for the center Notch shape from template A on page 138 onto the paper side of fusible web. Fold the sewn triangle down the center seam, wrong side out. Following manufacturer's instructions, fuse the notch shape to the wrong side of the folded rectangle unit. Cut the center notch shape out. Do not remove the paper yet.

5. Center the shape over the half-square triangle, with the lighter half of the notch shape on the dark triangle and the darker side of the notch shape on the light triangle. Remove the paper backing from the notch shape and fuse in place, carefully aligning the seamlines of the notch shape and the background square.

6. Following the directions for machine embroidery on page 67, stitch around the edges of the center shape. Test the stitch to get it to about ⅛"wide. I used a gold-colored rayon thread for the top and also for the bobbin. Carefully trim the blocks to 4 ½" (which includes the outer seam allowance).

Step I

Step 2

Step 3

Step 4

Step 5

Step 6

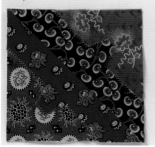

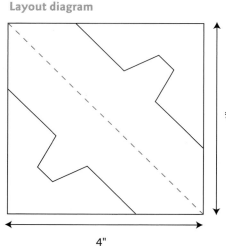

Layout diagram

4"

4"

COMPLETE BORDER

7. Sew the Elies blocks together into four sets of three and position around the center block. Add a Notch block to either end of each vertical set. Sew the horizontal then the vertical borders in place. For extra help on sewing the borders onto the quilt-in-progress, see page 81. Pieced borders like this one can be especially tricky. Use extra pins to hold the borders in place, avoiding stretch.

Second Pieced Border and Side Panels

This simple border consists of 24 small Elies blocks. The identical side panels are each made from seven blocks, for a total of 38 Elies blocks. You will very quickly develop a rhythm for making these blocks..

MATERIALS

Two-color background triangles: thirty-eight 6" squares in contrasting fabrics

Two-color center motifs: thirty-eight 4½" squares of contrasting fabrics

Fusible web

MAKING THE BORDER AND SIDE PANELS

1. Make 38 small Elies blocks, following the directions on page 65 to 66.

Steps 2 and 3 Border and side panels

2. Make two horizontal rows of five Elies blocks and sew to the top and bottom of the center medallion unit.

3. Make four vertical rows of seven Elies blocks. Sew together in into two pairs of vertical rows. Sew a pair to either side of the center medallion unit. Refer to page 81 for extra help with adding the borders. Your work-in-progress is now a rectangle.

Nine-Patch Elies Blocks & Checkerboard Blocks

Nine-patch clusters of Elies blocks separate the two pairs of checkerboards and enlarge the center field of the quilt. To save time, make up the blocks for these two clusters while you are making the other Elies blocks, and hold them until you have completed your checkerboards.

The checkerboards are made in two different color schemes (red/blue and red/cream), positioned diagonally opposite each other. The shapes of some of the appliqués vary from pair to pair. You will notice, too, that the bottom borders on the red/cream pairs is yet another variation. These appliqués sit on a pieced background. One wonders if two different soldiers made the two different sets of pairs, or if one man made all four blocks.

It is not difficult to make the checkerboards, but appliquéing the borders around them gets a bit fiddly, because the border strips are so narrow and the appliqué shapes are rather small. Still I love the look of the completed checkerboards. Wouldn't this make a great mini-wall-hanging? Or better still, make it as a gift for a chess or checkers lover—regular sized checkers are a perfect fit on these 2" squares!

MATERIALS

ELIES BLOCKS

> Two-color background triangles: eighteen 6" squares in contrasting fabrics
>
> Two-color center motifs: eighteen 4½" squares in contrasting fabrics
>
> Fusible web

CHECKERBOARD BLOCKS

> Red squares: ½ yard fabric
>
> White squares: ¼ yard fabric (not a fat quarter)
>
> Blue squares: ¼ yard fabric (not a fat quarter)
>
> Appliqués: fabric scraps in desired colors
>
> Border: ¼ yard cream fabric (not a fat quarter)
>
> Pieced bottom border: fabric scraps in desired colors
>
> Stabilizer and fusible web

Layout diagram

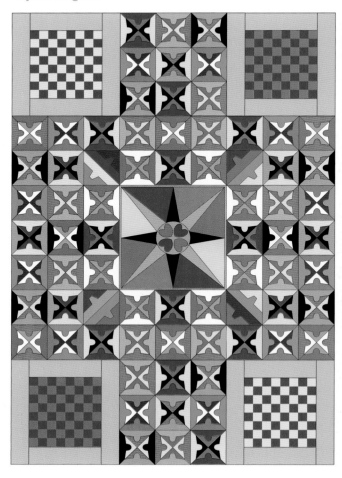

MAKING ELIES BLOCKS (MAKE 18)

Make 18 small Elies blocks, following the directions on pages 65 to 66. Sew into six horizontal rows of three blocks each. Complete the two clusters of nine blocks by sewing three rows together for each.

MAKING CHECKERBOARD (MAKE 4)

1. For the checkerboards, cut three 1½"-wide selvage-to-selvage strips each of blue and cream, plus six strips of red. For the borders, cut six 2½"-wide strips, selvage to selvage. Cut the border strips into twelve lengths, six of which are 8½" long (for top borders), and eight at 12½" long (for vertical borders). For the bottom borders of the red/cream checkerboard, cut eight 2½" squares each of cream plus eight 2½" squares in other desired colors.

2. Make three pairs of red and blue strips by sewing right sides together along one long side. Press the seam allowances to the blue strip.

3. Cut the three strips into 13" lengths. Sew four of these units together with an accurate ¼" seam, alternating red and blue bars.

4. Cut across the eight-bar unit to make eight 1½" strips.

5. Lay eight strips out so that red and blue squares alternate as shown, then stitch the strips together. Press the seam allowances open.

6. Repeat steps 1 to 4, this time using red and cream fabric strips.

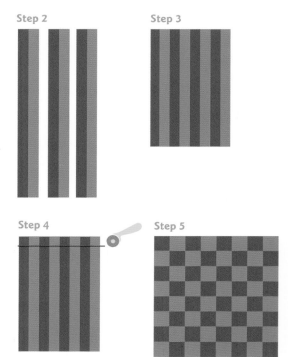

Step 2

Step 3

Step 4

Step 5

Layout diagram

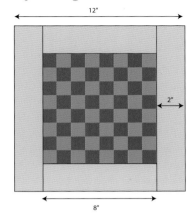

ADDING BORDERS TO CHECKERBOARDS

See template sets A (mini-pomegranate), B (small dot), C (diamond), D (dot), E (heart), F (small star), G (starburst), H (leaf), I (star on star), J (star), K (starburst with circles), and L (wend) on pages 139.

7. Follow the directions on pages 62 to 63 and page 67 to prepare, fuse, and machine embroider templates A to F onto the cream-colored vertical border strips (2½" x 12½"). Use the photographs as a guide. Note that the vertical borders are almost mirror images, but there are very slight differences between them. The quantities given on the template pieces will make two red/blue checkerboard borders plus two red/cream checkerboard borders.

8. In the same way, work with template sets G to K to complete the appliqués on the top/bottom border strips (2½" x 8½") of the red/blue checkerboard, plus the top border of the red/cream checkerboard. Examine the photos and the templates to identify differences between them and position each piece correctly. Note, for instance, that the heart in the border of the red/blue checkerboard is replaced by a circle in the border of the red/cream checkerboard.

Step 9

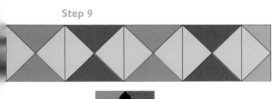

9. The background for the bottom border of the red/cream block is made up of three 2" Hourglass blocks, plus two half-Hourglass blocks. Follow steps I to 5 on pages 65 to 66 to make the blocks, starting with 2½" squares of fabric. Piece the Hourglass blocks together into a horizontal strip as shown. Follow the directions on pages 62 to 63 to prepare and fuse the wend motifs (template set L) on top of the pieced hourglass blocks.

10. Sew the 2½" x 8½" strips onto the top and bottom of the red/blue checkerboards and across the top of each red/cream checkerboard. Sew the pieced hourglass border to the bottom of each red/cream checkerboard. Sew the 2½" x 12½" strips to the sides of all four checkerboards.

11. Attach a square of stabilizer to the back of each bordered checkerboard.

COMPLETE

12. When two nine-patch Elies blocks and all four checkerboard blocks are complete, lay them out next to the work-in-progress. For the top row, a nine-patch block lies between a cream/red checkerboard on the left and a blue/red checkerboard on the right. For the bottom row, a nine-patch block lies between a blue/red checkerboard on the left and a red/cream checkerboard on the right.

13. Sew the three units comprising each row together, then sew the completed rows to the work-in-progress. The work is now a rectangle anchored by checkerboard blocks at each corner.

Hourglass and Pomegranate Side Panels

No patterns are required to make the Hourglass blocks. You have already made dozens of these if you have stitched the sections that require Elies blocks. However, Hourglasses are very attractive when used on their own, rather than as a component of another block, and are eye-catching choices for any project that calls for a colorful patchwork square. Each block is made up of two fabrics and only two seams.

This is the first time the full-size pomegranate motif has been used in the quilt, although it will become a very familiar component before the quilt is finished. There are thirteen in each of these two panels, for a total of twenty-six; you can sneak a look ahead to see how many are in the outer border. Because I alternated the placement of the light and medium-colored segments of the pomegranates, an impression of twining ribbon is achieved when the panel is finished.

MATERIALS

Hourglass blocks: Twenty-six 6" squares of contrasting fabrics

Pomegranate background, ½ yard of a good quality black fabric (see page 20 for a discussion of fabrics.)

Pomegranate centers: ½ yard of brown fabric

Side segments of pomegranates: ½ yard each of turkey red and antique cream fabrics

Pomegranate block circles: fat eighth each of antique blue and antique cream fabrics

Fusible web and stabilizer

MAKING THE HOURGLASS SIDE PANELS (MAKE 2)

1. Follow steps 2 to 5 of the directions for making Elies block on pages 65 to 66 to make a total of 26 Hourglass squares. Each is 4½" square, and will end up at 4" square when sewn into the quilt.

2. Divide the blocks into two piles of thirteen each. Sew the blocks end-to-end to make the panels, alternating the direction of the dark "hourglass" in each block so that it runs vertically in one block and horizontally in the one beneath.

3. Sew the panels to the center section of the quilt-in-progress, carefully aligning top and bottom edges.

In this in-progress photo, notice how the seams between the Hourglass blocks align exactly with the tips of the pomegranates in the next border.

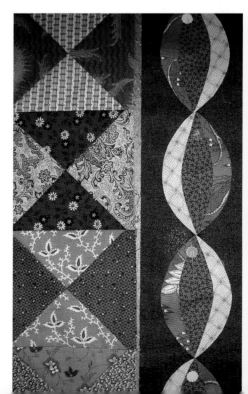

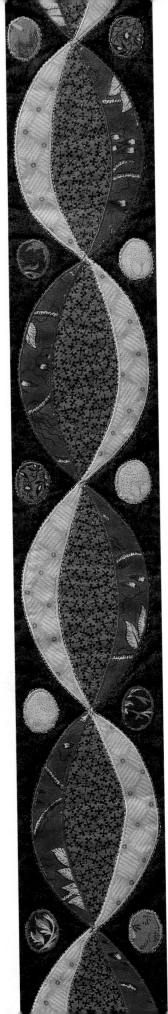

MAKING THE POMEGRANATE SIDE PANELS (MAKE 2)

See template A (pomegranate) and template B (dot) on page 138.

4. Following the directions for preparing motifs on pages 62 to 63, trace 26 pomegranate centers onto the paper side of the fusible web, adding a scant ¼" seam allowance. The two side segments of the pomegranates do not require seam allowances, as their edges will be hidden by the center piece. Trace the outer segments of the pomegranate in two groups of 26 so that half of them can be fused onto the turkey red fabric and the other half to the antique cream.

5. Trace 48 circles onto the paper side of the fusible web. Separate into two groups of 24 so that half of them can be fused onto the blue fabric and the other half onto the cream. Cut out all the pieces, keeping them organized.

6. From the black fabric, cut four strips of fabric 4½" x 27". From stabilizer, cut exact duplicates of the border strips.

7. Assemble the pomegranate shapes on a craft mat to aid in maintaining accuracy and consistency. Lay the center segment down, then place the side segments so that they overlap the seam allowances of the center segment. Fuse the three segments together to make one motif.

8. Seam two strips, right sides together, to make the required length for each side panel. This may be longer than you need, but I always make an appliqué panel longer than needed to start with, then cut it back to the correct length when the appliqué is completed.

9. Place the assembled pomegranates on the background strips beginning at the center of each strip—place the first pomegranate over the seam that joins the two sections of the background together, and make sure it is centered exactly on the width of the border. Stitch the first pomegranate in place. Continue to work from the center toward each end, turning the pomegranates so that the light and dark segments alternate and create that impression of twining ribbons. When the pomegranates are in position, embroider the cream side of all of them in a continuous seam, using matching thread: change to red thread and stitch the red sides in the same way. Next, position and embroider the circles, completing all same-color circles before changing thread for the next color.

10. When the appliqué is complete, it is time to trim the panels to size. The finished panel is 3 ½" wide and approximately 52" long. To determine the exact length, measure length-wise through the middle of the quilt-in-progress, and cut the panel to that length. It may work out that the amount you trim away should be divided between the ends of the panel strip—half off the top and half off the bottom, for example.

11. Pin the panels to the center section accurately. Begin by determining the horizontal center of the quilt and the halfway points between the center and the ends. Do the same on the panels. Match the horizontal center of each panel to the horizontal center of the quilt and pin; next, match ends, then the halfway point between each end and the center. Sew with an accurate ¼" seam.

Horizontal Appliqué Panels

These two borders provide our introduction to the many life forms featured on the quilt. There is a funny sort of deer that appears only in the bottom border; two kinds of butterflies; and a potted plant that resembles a succulent fruit. There are celestial objects and abstract shapes as well. The eleven motifs are used differently on the top and bottom borders. The motifs are cut from antique cream, blue, green, brown, tan and mustard, but can include almost any other fabric you have in your reproduction stash. If you decide to use solid fabrics, look for antique colors that will match the reproduction fabrics. You can use the leftovers from small print reproduction fabrics that you used for the Elies blocks.

MATERIALS

Background: ½ yard of good quality black fabric

Applique motifs: fat eighths in antique cream, blue, green, brown, tan, and mustard

Fusible web and stabilizer

MAKING THE APPLIQUÉ PANELS (MAKE 1 EACH)

See template sets A (star), B (potted plant), C (starburst), D (butterfly 1), E (moon cluster), F (floweret), G (butterfly 2), H (moon), I (freeform star), J (deer), K (doe) on pages 140 to 141.

1. Refer to the directions on preparing motifs on pages 62 to 63, and draw the required number of motifs on the paper side of the fusible web. Be sure to note when patterns must be reversed in order to have the final image going in the right direction. Group the patterns that will be cut from the same fabric near to one another to speed the fusing and cutting steps along.

2. From the black fabric, cut four strips of fabric 4 ½" x 26". From the stabilizer, cut exact duplicates of these background strips.

3. Seam two black strips, right sides together, to make the required length for each side panel. This is longer than you need, but I always make an appliqué panel longer than needed to start with, then cut it back to the correct length when the appliqué is completed. Place the stabilizer to the wrong side of the panel strips.

4. Place the assembled appliqués on the background strips beginning at the center of each strip—place the first shape over the seam that joins the two sections of the background together, and make sure it is centered exactly on the width of the border.

5. Work from the center outwards, embroidering each piece as you place it, and changing thread colors as required..

6. When the appliqué is complete, it is time to trim the borders to size. The finished border will be 3 ½" wide and approximately 50 ½" long. To determine the exact length, measure crosswise through the middle of the quilt-in-progress, and cut the border to

that length. It may work out that the amount you trim away can be divided between the ends of the border strip—half off the left end and half off the right end, for example.

7. Pin the borders to the quilt-in-progress accurately. Begin by determining the vertical center of the quilt and the halfway points between the center and the ends. Do the same on the borders. Match the vertical center of each panel to the vertical center of the quilt and pin; next, match ends, then the halfway point between each end and the center. Sew with an accurate ¼" seam.

Elies Block Side Panels

The final element of the colorful and multi-faceted square at the center of *1776* are the Elies block side panels. Though larger in size, these are made in exactly the same way as the smaller blocks closer to the center of the quilt. Each side panel consists of ten large Elies blocks sewn end-to-end

MATERIALS

Two-color background triangles: twenty 8" squares of contrasting fabrics

Two-color center motif: twenty 6" squares of contrasting fabric

Fusible web

MAKING THE ELIES SIDE PANELS (MAKE 2)

See template A on page 142.

1. Make 20 large Elies blocks, following the directions on pages 65 to 66.

2. Make two vertical rows of ten Elies blocks each.

3. Pin the panels to the center section accurately. Begin by determining the horizontal center of the quilt (which should be the seam in the background strip of the pomegranate border) and the halfway points between the center and the ends. Do the same on the panels. Match the horizontal center of each panel (which should be a seam between the fifth and sixth Elies blocks) to the horizontal center of the quilt and pin; next, match ends, then the halfway point between each end and the center. Sew with an accurate ¼" seam.

Chapter 7

Borders, Borders, Borders

I battle with borders until my head spins and provide directions for making each one

Most striking in *1776* are the borders upon borders upon borders that surround the quilt center. Some are pieced, some are appliquéd, some are narrow, and others wide. It is often said of wall art that the frame makes the picture. That being so, what a wonderful framing these miraculous borders add to *1776*.

Cream Appliqué Border

The first full appliqué border really stands out in *1776*. A major reason is the light, cream-colored background that contrasts with the medium-to-dark tones of the backgrounds of other borders in the quilt. Quite a number of fascinating new motifs make an appearance on this round of the quilt. I really enjoyed working out the appliqués for them.

Notice that the motifs in the horizontal borders include images of people going about a number of activities. An infantryman proudly marches along with his gun on his shoulder and huge sword at his side. A soldier/musician mysteriously balances a large viola on his wrist. Two men with bottles may be soldiers celebrating some time off with a bit of wine.

MATERIALS

Background: 2 ½ yards of light-colored fabric

Appliqué motifs: scraps (use solid colors for the animal figures)

Fusible web and stabilizer

MAKING THE BORDER

For horizontal borders, see template sets A (bird in tree), B (marching soldier), C (fronds), D (bottom jumping dog), E (top jumping dog), F (bird on branch), G (boar), H (deer with horns), I (rabbit), J (musician), K (flower), L (balloon tree) on pages 143 to 147. For vertical borders, see template sets M (starburst and balloons), N (three crosses), O (compass), P (shade tree), Q (potted fronds and deer), R (birds and deer), S (moonflower and deer), T (star and balloons), U (three diamonds) on pages 145 to 150.

1. Follow the directions on preparing motifs on pages 62 to 63, then trace the patterns for the two vertical panels onto the paper side of the fusible web. Note that each motif must be traced two times, since the images in the side borders match, as do those in the top/bottom borders. Notice that some top/bottom border motifs need to be reversed and traced two more times, as they appear on both sides of the center motif, the "balloon tree" that shelters the two drinking men. Group together the motifs, or sections of motifs, that will be cut from the same fabric to facilitate cutting and fusing.

2. From the light-colored fabric, cut nine strips 8" x 31." Four of these strips will be used for the background of the side borders, and five will be needed for the background of the top and bottom borders. From the stabilizer, cut exact duplicates of the background strips.

3. Seam two background strips, right sides together, to make the required length for each side border. This is longer than you need, but I always make an appliqué panel longer than needed to start with, then cut it back to the correct length when the appliqué is completed. Place the stabilizer to the wrong side of the panel strips.

4. Prepare strips for the top/bottom borders in the same way. Cut one of the 8" x 31" strips in half to obtain an 8" x 15 ½" strip. Each border requires one of these halves, plus two 31" strips. Seam the strips, right sides together to make a strip measuring 8" x 77 ½". Place the half length between the two full lengths in order to keep a graceful balance of seam-lines. Press the seams open. Place the stabilizer to the wrong side of the panel strips.

5. Place the assembled appliqué motifs on the background strips beginning at the center of each strip—place the first motif over the seam that joins the two sections of the background together, and make sure it is centered exactly on the width of the border. See the section on machine appliqué on pages 63 to 63 and page 67 to fuse then machine embroider the first motif in place. Continue to work from the center toward each end, embroidering each motif as you place it.

6. When the appliqué is complete, it is time to trim the borders to size. Each finished border will be 6½" wide finished, so it must be cut back to 7." The side borders will be approximately 59 ½" long; the top/bottom borders will be approximately 73½" long.

Narrow Three-Part Border

No patterns are required for the narrow set of three borders that surrounds the first full appliqué border. All you need is three strips of fabric—two of red and one of gold. The three borders actually read as one solid stripe of color around the center section of the quilt. I sewed each strip onto the quilt individually, rather than piecing the three strips together and then sewing the unit onto the quilt. In retrospect, these narrow borders may be easier to handle if you combine them first.

¾" selvage to selvage

1" selvage to selvage

1 ½" selvage to selvage

MATERIALS

½ yard turkey-red fabric

½ yard gold or mustard fabric

MAKING THE BORDER

1. From the red fabric, cut nine ¾"-wide selvage-to-selvage strips for the innermost border and nine 1½"-wide selvage-to-selvage strips for the outermost border. From the gold or mustard fabric, cut nine 1"-wide selvage-to-selvage strips for the middle border.

2. Sew the fabric strips for each border together into a three-strip-unit.

3. Follow the directions on page 81 to accurately measure for, cut, then attach the border units to the quilt. Press all seam allowances to the borders.

Measuring, Cutting, & Attaching Borders

On a quilt with so many borders, it is extremely important to make sure that the strips you add are exactly the right size for your quilt. The directions for most borders provide approximate border lengths or selvage-to-selvage cutting requirements, but you must follow these instructions to guarantee accuracy.

1. To determine the exact length for each vertical border, measure lengthwise through the middle of the quilt, and cut the border to that length, as shown.

2. Matching raw edges and right sides together, pin the side borders to the quilt-in-progress.

Begin by determining the horizontal center of the quilt and place one or two pins. Smooth the border out with your hand, then place pins at either end. Find the halfway points between the center and the ends and pin again. Go back to the center, then pin at 6" intervals, all along the raw edges, smoothing out the fabric with your hand as you go. This way, the stretch of the fabric is equal across the quilt, and any extra length is eased in at intervals along the entire border. Sew with an accurate ¼" seam.

3. Repeat Steps 1 and 2 to measure then attach the top/bottom borders to the quilt in the same way.

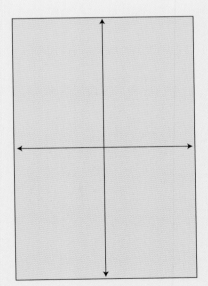

Measure horizontally and vertically through the middle of the quilt

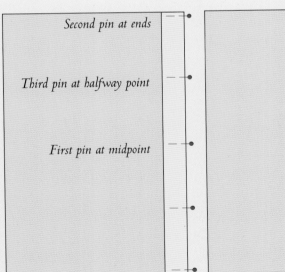

Second pin at ends

Third pin at halfway point

First pin at midpoint

Place border and pin

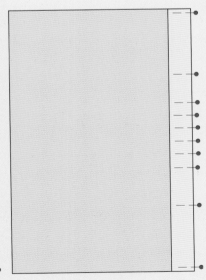

Pin every 6" up and down the edge

Date Panels

In these two panels, the infantry is joined by the cavalry. Can there be any doubt that the makers of this quilt were drawing inspiration from their daily lives? Maybe they even saw a partridge in a pear tree, since there is one in each corner! The borders are exactly the same except for the dates: the one in the top reads "1776" and the bottom reads "1779". I imagine they indicate either the span of time the soldiers were at a certain posting, or the beginning and ending years for the making of the quilt—or maybe both.

MATERIALS

Background: 1¾ yards of black or dark slate grey fabric

Horses: ¼ yard of solid dusty blue fabric

Soldiers, crest, lettering, and one horse: ¾ yard of cream fabric

Uniforms, boots, hats, etc: one fat quarter each of mustard, tan, olive green

Other motifs: ½ yard of solid turkey red fabric

Fusible web and stabilizer

MAKING THE PANELS (MAKE TWO)

See template sets A (partridge in a pear tree), B (infantryman), C (cavalryman), D (date), E (shield) on pages 151 to 154.

1. Follow the directions for preparing motifs on pages 62 to 63 to trace the patterns for the two borders onto the paper side of the fusible web. Note that the infantryman must be traced eight times, then the pattern reversed and traced eight more times. The soldier on horseback must be traced four times, then reversed and traced another four times. The partridge in the pear tree is repeated four times. The shield and date appears twice, but the numbers "6" and "9" only once each (turn the "6" upside down to create the "9"). Group together the motifs, or sections of motifs, that will be cut from the same fabric to facilitate fusing and cutting. (In each panel, I made two of my partridges white, and two of them gold. I also made one solid white horse, while the others are blue with white tails.)

2. From the black or dark slate gray fabric, cut six 9"-wide strips across the width of the fabric. From the stabilizer, cut exact duplicates of the background strips.

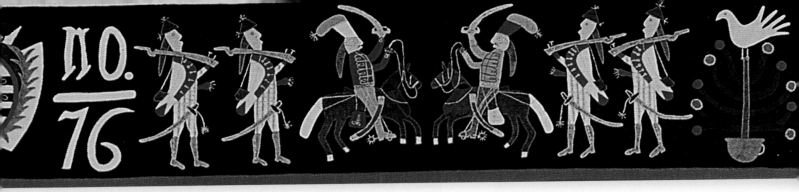

3. Sew the fabric strips for the borders together. To determine the length you need, measure through the horizontal center of the quilt. Add ½" for seam allowances. The strips should be approximately 80" long after seaming. Place the stabilizer to the wrong side of the panel strips.

4. Place the assembled appliqué motifs on the background strips beginning at the center of each strip, making sure it is also centered exactly on the width of the border. Follow the directions on pages 62 to 63 and page 67 to fuse then machine-embroider the first motif in place. Continue to work from the center toward each end, embroidering each motif as you place it.

5. When the appliqué is complete, it is time to trim the panels to size. Each finished panel will be 8" wide, so each must be cut back to 8½". It will be approximately 79" long. Follow the directions on page 81 to achieve accurate measurements and attach the borders.

Extra-Narrow Cream Border

This ¼" border is so narrow that it is easy to overlook; however, it adds just the right degree of separation between the different elements of the quilt. It is fiddly to work with such long, narrow strips, but your perseverence will pay off in the end.

MATERIALS

½ yard of good quality cream-colored fabric

MAKING THE BORDER

1. Cut twelve ¾"-wide strips across the width of the fabric.

2. Sew the fabric strips for the border together, end-to-end. To determine the length you need, measure through the center of the quilt, both lengthwise and crosswise. Add ½" to those lengths for seam allowances. Sew the borders first to the sides of the quilt, then to the bottom and top. Press the seam allowances to the border, which will finish ¼" wide.

Appliqué Block Border

The 56 blocks of this next-to-last appliqué border include three motifs in a new style that I call *layered geometric*. Quite simply, the shapes that make up the design are stacked, fused, and stitched on top of one another in layers. One of these blocks, the Wendish block, is very similar to the familiar Log Cabin block; the other two, the Sorbian and Bautzen blocks are forms of bulls-eyes. The names I have given them speak to the heritage of the quilt. Most of the blocks measure 6" x 6" when complete, but there is some variation in the width from block to block.

Within the forty-four appliquéd blocks that contain plant or animal life, there are some new images. A pair of storks make their home in a twig nest; the larger one prepares to deliver a baby bundle. Two new trees show many kinds of blossoms, ignoring the rules of botany. A guard stands next to a barricade. Then, like a tightrope walker, he is on top of the barricade, performing acrobatics. The cavalry is back in force on the side borders, and a new type of soldier makes an appearance on the top and bottom borders; appearing in pairs, the red-cloaked figures appear to be smoking giant pipes, but they could also musicians with alpine horns. The double-headed eagle, long a national symbol of Germany, appears four times.

With the amount of blocks in these four borders you could almost make a single bed quilt! Notice that no prints are used in this border, only solid-color fabrics.

MATERIALS

Background squares: ¼ yard each of cream, dark blue, dusty green, dusty blue, dusty mint green, black, dusty lilac, and turkey red fabrics

Appliques: scraps of fabrics listed above

Tracing paper or ¼ yard lightweight (sheer) interfacing (for Bautzen blocks only)

Fusible web and stabilizer

MAKING THE TOP/BOTTOM BORDERS (MAKE TWO)

See template sets A (flower tree), B (eagle), C (cactus tree), D (soldier with pipe), E (potted tree), and F (guard at barricade) on pages 155 to 157. Note: for one F block and one reverse F block, position guard atop barricade.

I. Follow the directions on preparing motifs on pages 62 to 63 to trace the patterns for the top and bottom border motifs onto the paper side of the fusible web. There are a total of seven different motifs. Notice that the patterns are reversed for half the blocks. The exception is the guard block/guard on barricade blocks: the pattern is not reversed, but the guard on the right is atop, not beside the barricade. Group together the motifs, or sections of motifs, that will be cut from the same fabric to facilitate fusing and cutting.

2. The top and bottom borders each require a pair (reverse for one) of the following blocks. Cut fabrics and same-size squares of stabilizer for the backgrounds as follows:

> Flower tree block: 4 dusty green backgrounds, 7" (when complete, trim to 6" x 5¾")
>
> Eagle block: 4 dusty lilac backgrounds, 7½" (when complete, trim to 6" x 7")
>
> Cactus tree block: 4 mint green backgrounds, 7" (when complete, trim to 6" x 5¾")
>
> Soldiers with pipes block: 4 black backgrounds, 8" (when complete, trim to 6" x 7¾")
>
> Potted tree block: 4 dusty blue backgrounds, 7" (when complete, trim to 6" x 5¾")
>
> Guard block/guard on barricade block: 2 dark blue and 2 turkey red backgrounds, 7" (when complete, trim to 6" x 5¾")

3. Fuse then machine-embroider the assembled motifs in place on the background squares. Trim each completed block to the size indicated in Step 2.

4. Join the blocks as shown in the photograph to complete the top and bottom borders.

MAKING THE VERTICAL BORDERS (MAKE ONE EACH)

See template sets G (storks), H (Bautzen block), I (Sorbian block), and J (Wendish block) on pages 156 to 158. See also, template set C (cavalryman) from Date Panel on page 153.

1. Follow the directions on preparing motifs on pages 62 to 63 to trace the patterns for the vertical border motifs onto the paper side of the fusible web. There are a total of just five different motifs, though the soldier on horseback appears eight times in each border, in a variety of color schemes. The other four motifs appear twice in each border, for a total of 16 blocks per border. Notice that the patterns are reversed for half the blocks. The solders on horseback must be traced a total of sixteen times, eight for the left border and eight for the right border. I made some of my horses black, others cream-colored. Group together the motifs, or sections of motifs, that will be cut from the same fabric to facilitate fusing and cutting.

2. The vertical borders each require a pair of the following blocks, reversing the pattern for the right-hand border as shown in the photograph. Cut fabrics and same-size squares of stabilizer for the backgrounds as follows:

> Stork block: 4 black backgrounds, 7" (when complete, trim to 6" x 6")
>
> Sorbian horseman block: 10 dusty blue backgrounds, 4 dark blue backgrounds, 2 dusty green background, 7½" (when complete, trim to 6" x 6¼")
>
> Sorbian block: 3 turkey red backgrounds, 2 cream backgrounds, 1 black background, 7" (when complete, trim to 6" x 6½")
>
> Wendish block: 2 cream backgrounds, 7" (when complete, trim to 6" x 6¼")
>
> Bautzen block: scraps (when complete, trim to 6" x 6")

3. Fuse then machine-embroider the assembled motifs for the stork blocks and Sorbian horseman blocks onto the background squares. Trim each completed block to the size indicated in Step 2.

4. You may choose from two ways to make the Bautzen and Sorbian blocks. Using a very lightweight fusible web to avoid bulk, you can build the layers by simply fusing the largest shape onto the background, fusing the next-largest on top of that, and so on, ending with the circle and the on-point square at the center of each of these blocks. If you are concerned about bulk, simply trim away the inner portion of each layer (i.e., the portion that will not show), about 1" from the edge. Then fuse in place as usual. The shapes will nestle inside each other. There is no need to trim the circle or the on-point square at the center.

5. To make the Wendish block, begin by tracing or photocopying the template diagram on page 159 (including all lines and numbers) onto see-through interfacing or tracing paper. Setting your machine to 16 to 18 stitches per inch, perforate the paper or interfacing along all marked lines. Add ¼" all round to fabric pieces 1 to 25.

   Place fabric piece 1 with the right side facing up on the unmarked side of the paper or interfacing. Hold the entire block up to the light to make sure you have covered piece 1 adequately, then pin to hold. Prepare and position piece 2 in the same way. Paper side up and fabric side down, position the block on the sewing machine and sew along the first line (between pieces 1 and 2), beginning ¼" before and ending ¼" after the marked line. Remove from the machine, press, then trim the seam back by ¼" at either end. Pick up piece 3, and repeat. Continue until all 25 pieces are sewn in place, then press and trim the block to 6" x 6". Appliqué the diamond to the center.

6. Join the blocks for each border as shown in the photographs.

Assembly

7. Pin the horizontal and vertical borders to the quilt-in-progress accurately. Follow the directions on page 81 to accurately measure for and attach the vertical then the horizontal borders.

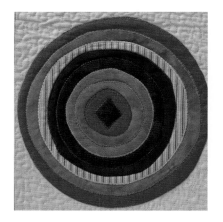

Pomegranate Border

There are 94 pomegranate appliqués, in 52 color schemes, and 196 berries (or circles) in this part of the quilt. I actually made 100 pomegranates and 200 berries. They seemed to multiply almost by themselves.

MATERIALS

Background: 1½ yards dark fabric or assorted dark fabrics

Side segments of pomegranates: 1 yard cream fabric or combination of creams; 1 yard of dusty blue fabric or combination of blues and lavenders

Center segments of pomegranates: fat quarters of turkey-red, rust, dusty green, dark blue, and gray fabrics

Corner blocks: scraps of pomegranate fabrics

Fusible web and stabilizer

MAKING THE BORDER (MAKE FOUR PANELS)

See template set A (pomegranate—prepare 94) and template set B (dot—prepare 196) for first pomegranate border on page 138 and template set A (small Sorbian block) on page 159.

1. Follow the directions for preparing motifs on pages 62 to 63 to trace 94 pomegranate centers onto the paper side of the fusible web, adding a scant ¼" seam allowance. The two side segments of the pomegranates do not require seam allowances, as they will overlap the center. Trace the outer segments of the pomegranate in two groups of 47 so that half of them can be fused onto the cream-colored fabric and the other half to the blue (or the blue/violet mix).

2. Trace 196 circles onto the paper side of the fusible web. Separate into groups according to the number you want of each color to facilitate fusing and cutting.

3. The background strip should be cut 5" wide. To determine the length you need, measure through the center of the quilt, both lengthwise and crosswise (see also page 81). If you are using one continuous strip, cut it to this length plus about 6". If you are piecing the background, cut twelve strips of different colors and lengths; seam them together end-to-end. Cut the pieced strip to the lengths you need for the two side panels and the top and bottom borders, adding about 6" to each strip. From the stabilizer, cut exact duplicates of the background strips.

4. For the corner blocks, cut 3½" squares of background. Following the directions for fusible appliqué on pages 62 to 63 and using template set A (corner block), layer the circles to complete the block.

5. Assemble the pomegranate shapes, working on a craft mat to aid in maintaining accuracy and consistency. Lay the center segment down right side up, then place the side segments so that they overlap the seam allowances of the segment. Following the directions that come with the fusible web, fuse the segments together.

6. Assemble the four motifs for the corner blocks, fusing them together in layers.

7. Place stabilizer on the wrong side of the border background strips. I have a few hints for placing the pomegranates on the border background. First, establish the exact length of the borders on the background strips by marking each end of the strip with a white pencil. (Remember to add a ¼" seam allowance beyond the end of the strip.) These end marks will give you a guide as to where the pomegranate appliqués need to start and finish. Next, mark the center line of the strip, again with a white pencil; since the border strip is 5" wide at this point, the center line of the quilt is 2½" from the long edges. This is where the points of the pomegranates must go.

8. Place the assembled pomegranate motifs on the background strips, using your marks to space them accurately. You may find it helpful to place the first motif at the middle of the border strip, then work toward each end. Although it would be nice if the tips of the pomegranates always touched, that may not be possible if the background strip is a bit longer than the combined length of the pomegranates. In that case, you must fiddle with the placement until the pomegranates are evenly spaced.

9. Following the directions on pages 62 to 63 and page 67, fuse then machine-embroider the first motif in place. Continue to work from the center toward each end, embroidering each pomegranate. When the appliqués are complete, sew a corner square to both ends of the top and bottom borders.

10. When the appliqués are complete, it is time to trim the borders to size. The finished border will be 3 ½" wide, so it must be cut back to 4." Trim the ends of the four borders to fit the lengths required for the two sides and the two top and bottom borders. It may work out that the amount you trim away should be divided between the ends of the panel strip—half off each end.

11. Follow the directions on page 81 to measure for and attach the borders.

Final Border

A solid Turkey red border finishes off the quilt, and it is simple to make. With it, you will have finished the top. Imagine my delight when I reached this stage, after many long days and nights of working on the quilt. Congratulations, you have completed the final border!

MATERIALS

2 ¼ yards of solid turkey red fabric

MAKING THE BORDER (MAKE FOUR BORDER STRIPS)

1. Cut sixteen 3 ½" wide strips of fabric.

2. Sew the fabric strips for the border together, end-to-end.

3. Follow the directions on measuring for and attaching borders on page 81 to sew the borders to the quilt.

Finishing the Quilt

You may use any basic reference book on quilting to learn how to add batting and backing, layer, quilt, and bind your quilt. To read of my experiences and tips for finishing a large quilt like *1776*, refer to pages 50 to 52. The choices I made for quilting *1776* are described in my journal (see page 55). You are free to follow my suggestions or create quilting designs of your own.

BINDING *1776*

A beautifully finished quilt depends on a well-constructed binding. Fortunately, this is not difficult to accomplish. When I completed the quilting of *1776*, I had difficulty deciding just what binding I should use. I love multi-colored bindings, but I had almost run out of long

pieces of fabric. I decided to use the leftover fabrics in the stash. I prefer a 3" wide binding strip, because it will finish the edge beautifully and give you a very flat finish.

1. Trim the quilt to the exact size. If you have measured carefully as you added each border to the quilt, and made sure the quilt was square at each stage of construction, it should be square when it is finished. Measure through the center of the quilt vertically and horizontally. Then measure the sides of the quilt and note any difference from the center measurement; measure the top and bottom edges and note any deviation from the center horizontal measurement. Lay the quilt flat and trim carefully with a ruler and rotary cutter.

2. Measure the diameter of the quilt to determine what the length of the binding should be; add about 18" extra to allow for mitering corners and finishing the ends. Cut 3"-wide binding strips across the width of the fabric, in a quantity to accomplish the length you require.

3. Fold the entire length of the strip in half, wrong sides together. Press.

4. Measure the bottom edge of the quilt and determine the center. Measure a length of binding to equal half the width of the bottom edge, plus about 6"; mark with a pin.

Lay the cut edge of the binding on the cut edge of the quilt, leaving a "tail" of about 6" at the center of the quilt. Match the pin on the binding to the first corner (the bottom left) and pin the binding to the quilt. Place additional pins every 6" along the binding. Repeat this process on all four sides of the quilt: measure the length of the quilt, measure the binding, pin the center of the length of binding to the center of the length of the side, then pin the corners. Work out to the corners from the center with additional pins every 6".

5. Using the side of the walking foot as a guide, carefully sew on the binding. (This will give you a seam allowance of approximately 3⅜".)

6. Fold the binding to the back of the quilt and pin in place. I pin just a short distance at a time and sew it down before going to the next section. I like to use long, thin, flower head pins, because they are sharp enough to go through the three layers easily (four layers, if you count the actual appliqués.)

7. Hand-sew the binding in place on all four sides of the quilt, using a small, invisible stitch and thread that blends with the fabric.

8. Gently form the mitered corners as you come to each. Sew a small running stitch up into the corner to hold the miter firm.

9. Finger-press a crease where the binding will end and cut it back, allowing a ¼" seam.

10. Sew the seam by hand and press the seam open. Complete the stitching that holds the binding in place.

LABEL

Turn over your quilt and add a label! The story of *1776* is printed onto fabric then fused to the back of the quilt.

Bright Baby 1776 by Jenny Loveder (27" x 44")

PART THREE

OFFSPRING QUILTS

Projects Inspired by 1776

Chapter 8

A Bounty of Inspiration

My quilting friends, The Retreating Angels, show how versatile the motifs in 1776 can be, with quilts of their own design

Buatzen's *1776* is astounding in the utter abundance of original motifs displayed across its surface. Two distinctive examples of patchwork are found in the Elies and Notch blocks and three never-before-seen abstract appliqués appear in the Sorbian, Bautzen, and Wendish blocks.

Perhaps most fascinating, though, are the appliquéd vignettes depicting realistic subjects that seized the attention of the soldier quiltmakers. These fabric snapshots undoubtedly reflect actual objects or activities surrounding the stitchers. The appliqué motifs range from varied and assorted manifestations of heavenly bodies, to a broad array of flora and fauna, some of which are quite fanciful, to humans engaged in different pursuits, mainly soldiering. (Women are notably absent.) The motifs are sometimes combined in whimsical ways, appearing to suggest a story. They are true examples of naïve art (also known as folk art), the term used to describe art made by persons who have had no professional training in painting, drawing, sculpture, or other of the visual arts. Folk art, no matter what country it comes from, whether America, Ghana, Brazil, Thailand, or Germany, always seems to strike a chord with the viewer. That is what makes this quilt so very appealing.

PREVIOUS PAGE:
"Using botanicals in the brightest fabrics I could find, I hand-appliquéd my motifs to a black background. They just sparkled! I hand-quilted around the shapes and bound the top with bright stripes. I just love this quilt!" Jenny Loveder

The Retreating Angels

I was thrilled when my quilting group, the Retreating Angels (so named because a retreat bought us all together and our logo is an angel), agreed to make small quilts for this book. Each of the Retreating Angels is a talented quilter in her own right and has exhibited her work either locally, nationally, or internationally, and several have designed quilts for national magazines. Since 1999, we have had regular retreats and cooperated on group projects.

Angst notwithstanding, the Angels demonstrated just how versatile the motifs from 1776 are. The women changed the sizes of the motifs to suit the dimensions of their individual projects; they experimented with myriad color schemes; they combined the motifs into inventive groupings. About the only thing our fourteen creations (one quilt is done in two colorways) have in common is the same "folk art" feeling of the original quilt. Our versions are only the beginning of countless possibilities, and we hope that our efforts will encourage you to enjoy the motifs from 1776 in a project of your own.

The Retreating Angels have been stitching together for more than a decade. Left to right, back row: Heather Bolt, Dianne Assheton, Liz Needle, Jane Green; middle row: Elvira Richardson, Jenny Loveder, Vera Lloyd, Mary Heard, Pam Holland; front: Jan Munzberg. Missing: Chris O' Brien and Clare Warby,

A Gallery of Quilts

Welcome Home, by Mary Heard (48" x 48")

"When the Retreating Angels were challenged by Pam Holland to make smaller designs derived from her prizewinning quilt, I developed this pattern. I saw the checkerboards in The 1776 Quilt as a town square. Here, the soldiers are either on parade or perhaps leaving for the battlefield. The excitement created by all the noise and movement is reflected in the figures in the border." Mary Heard

A Glimpse of Heartache, Heritage, & Happiness by Jan Munzberg
(27 ½" x 27 ½")

"It was a treat and a challenge to work with Pam, a gifted designer and a generous teacher, to create just a glimpse of Heartache, Heritage and Happiness. My goals for my project were to show one design made up in two very different color schemes, (see quilt on page 100).
I also wanted to have a little joke by inserting a kangaroo, which is not among the motifs from the original quilt. The motifs I used were the Elies block, the central plant with bird, and all those other wonderful animals."
Jan Munzberg

1776 Revisited, by Vera Lloyd
(37" x 46")

"I made my quilt in tribute to the beautiful *1776* by Pam Holland. Although I adapted two of the patchwork blocks—the Elies and the Notch—for use in my quilt, I duplicated exactly the soldier on horseback."
Vera Lloyd

Partridge in a Pear Tree, by Jan Munzberg (35" x 38")

"This quilt was a labor of love instigated by the Retreating Angels. Pam Holland generously shared her designs from the stunning *1776: Heartache, Heritage, and Happiness* quilt. Using EQ5, this is the "offspring quilt" I designed. I enjoyed yet another learning experience from Pam as I designed and created my own quilt." Jan Munzberg

Honoring the Past, by Chris O'Brien
(60" x 60")

"Because I have always had a passion for investigating aspects of the past, it was the opportunity to spend time reflecting on the makers of the original *1776* that provided such pleasure as I made my own small version. I pondered the materials the soldiers used, the conditions in which they worked, and the motivations which guided their endeavors. I came to feel that we are blessed to be guided in our creative work today by the masterpieces of those quilters who came before us." Chris O'Brien

Penny Rug, by Jane Green
(32" x 44")

"Because my family and I live in a fourth-generation orchard, I named the quilt store I opened in 1994 The Patchwork Apple. The name also indicates my love of the country look, especially traditional patterns and fabrics. I adore things that have lived elsewhere—rustic furniture, old quilts, and antiques. My collection of folk art from the United States and Europe inspired me to adapt the motifs from *The 1776 Quilt* to an old-fashioned penny rug." Jane Green

Two More Offspring Quilts

During the same time when the Retreating Angels were working on their projects, I was wondering what sort of "offspring" a man might make. It would be very interesting, I thought, to see how 21st-century men might work with motifs developed by other men three centuries earlier. I had the occasion to issue a challenge to two men in Grayling, Michigan, during a teaching tour at the Ice House Quilt Shop. I was a guest of Dave and Jill Wyman, whose daughter owns the quilt shop; their friends, Ed and Jan Bryan, happened to be visiting at the same time.

One evening after supper, I showed the group my *1776* and related its story. All listened with interest, and early the next morning, I found the two men poring over the quilt, examining it in minute detail.

Dave had made a quilt previously, having enrolled in several classes at his daughter's shop. Ed declared that he would like to make a quilt one day. So I leapt at the opportunity to suggest that they each make a wall hanging based on *1776*.

They accepted the dare, and several months later, two beautifully executed small quilts arrived in the post. Fine details abound in each, but that did not surprise me at all. I had faith that these two very motivated men would show us all that anyone can, with solid determination, achieve their goal.

" *1776* can only be described as 'awesome.' I admired the design, workmanship, and authentic story of the quilt. When Pam asked me to make an original piece for her book using the *1776* patterns, I was delighted. It was a joy to study the motifs on the original quilt and decide which ones I would use on my piece. I liked choosing the fabrics, as well as cutting and piecing the project. Nancy Webster of Northwoods Quilting did the machine quilting, and I was so happy with her creativity." Dave Wyman

"I made my quilt top from fabrics I picked from my wife's stash (much to her consternation) and from others I found in local quilt shops. After I had seen it, Pam sent me several patterns from her *1776* quilt. With the help of my master-quilter wife, Jan Bryan, I sewed all the pieces together, but then I ran out of time to complete the quilting. I sent it out to Michelle Rozelle, whose machine quilting I have long admired, because quilting is a major part of my wall hanging. This is the first quilt I have ever made, and I thought, 'Wow! This can become addicting.'" Ed Bryan

Quick List of Techniques

This easy-reference checklist will help you find directions for techniques used in each of the patterns. It may also be helpful to you when you begin making quilts of your own design using the motifs or methods designed for my version of *1776*.

Supplies	*Pages 20 to 23*	*Pomegranate border*	*Page 75 and*
Hourglass block	*Pages 65 to 66*		*pages 87 to 90*
Elies block	*Pages 65 to 66*	*Borders*	*Pages 81*
Notch block	*Pages 68 to 69*	*Quilt "sandwich"*	*Page 50*
Machine appliqué	*Pages 62 to 63*	*Machine quilting*	*Pages 52 to 55*
Machine embroidery	*Page 67*	*Binding*	*Pages 90 to 91*
Checkerboard	*Pages 70 to 73*	*Label*	*Page 93*
Foundation pieced Wendish block	*Page 86*	*Resizing motifs*	*Page 105*

Special Sewing Machine Supplies

See pages 22 to 23 for detailed descriptions of the tools and fabrics I used in making *1776*. In the meantime, here is a short list of special sewing machine equipment that will make your work easier.

Machine needles, size 60/8 sharps

Open-toed foot for appliqué

Embroidery or free-motion foot for free-hand quilting

Walking foot for quilting

Quilt Patterns

Following are six patterns for small quilts that incorporate motifs from *1776*. I hope they will inspire you to take your own trip back into time with my Prussian soldiers. Before you get started, though, here are some suggestions on how to work.

SIZING THE MOTIFS

Many of the motifs were used same-size in the projects the Retreating Angels made. However, in other cases, one Angel wanted to enlarge a particular motif to use as the center of her medallion-style piece; another two or three Angels reduced an appliqué motif to fit onto a narrow border; in other examples, the Angel required an Elies block even smaller than the 4" block for which a pattern is given.

In each of these cases, the Angel obtained the desired size by simply scanning the motif as it appears in the templates section of this book into a computer, then using computer tools to enlarge or reduce as needed. Sizing by computer significantly reduces the time it takes to produce a pattern of the dimensions you require for your particular project. If you do not have the capacity to do this at home, I suggest that you take your pattern to a local copy shop where it can easily and inexpensively be made to the size you need. It may facilitate scanning if you first trace your motifs from the book onto single sheets of paper. (Review the instructions for machine appliqué on pages 62 to 63.)

USING THE TEMPLATES

With the exception of the piecing templates for the center square on page 136 and the Wendish block on page 161, all the templates are designed for machine fusing, which does not require seam allowance. Following the directions for machine appliqué on page 62 to 63, you will need to trace each element of each template set individually onto fusible web, in the quantities specified. With complex template sets like the soldiers (for instance, on page 153), this is fiddly work. Be sure to prepare each piece, then lay them on an appliqué mat to make sure they match to template set and the photograph. Note that the dashed lines on the templates sets indicate machine embroidery.

1776 Heritage Quilt Sampler

*I chose a single motif for the center
of my quilt, surrounded by Elies blocks*

I designed this small quilt specifically to use some of the techniques I developed during the making of *1776*. The lessons this small quilt teaches are machine appliqué, how to make the Elies block, and how to blend reproduction fabrics.

MATERIALS

Background of center panel and fourth border: 1 fat quarter cream fabric

Wide fourth border: ¾ yard light tan fabric

Pieced border of Elies blocks, plus corner squares: 12 fat quarters of reproduction fabric

Center appliqué: 5 fat eighths of different green fabrics

Vase, bird, and berries: scraps in desired colors

Narrow first and third borders: ¼ yard (not a fat quarter) of dark color

Backing: 1 yard cotton in desired color

Binding: 1 yard

Thin cotton batting: 1 yard

Fusible web and stabilizer

Finished size: 31" x 31" plus binding

TEMPLATES

For Elies blocks, use template A (small Elies block) on page 138 (prepare 16). For center motif, use offspring template A (bird in tree) on page 160 (prepare 1).

CUTTING

1. From the cream fabric, cut a 12" square for the background of the center block. From the light tan, cut four 5½" x 32" strips for the fourth border.

2. From the 12 fat quarters of reproduction fabrics, cut sixteen 6"squares and sixteen 4½" squares. Cut eight 5½" squares, half in cream and half in turkey red, for the corner blocks in the fourth border.

3. From the dark-colored fabric for the first and third borders, cut four 1" wide strips across the width of the fabric. You will use two for each border.

4. For the square-on-square corner motifs, cut four 3⅝" squares of reproduction or pictorial fabric, centering a desired motif on the squares.

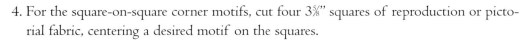

Layout diagram

CUTTING AND ASSEMBLING APPLIQUÉ PATTERNS

5. Trace the center motif (bird in tree) onto fusible web. Following the directions on pages 62 to 63 and page 67, prepare, fuse, and machine-embroider the motif in place on the center square. When the embroidery is complete, press the block and trim it to exactly 11½" square.

SEWING AND APPLIQUE

6. For the first narrow border around the center square, use two of the 1"wide fabric strips in the dark-colored fabric. Cut two 11½" lengths, then pin one to the top and one to the bottom of the block. Sew in place. Press the seam allowances carefully toward the border. Measure the block vertically through the center and cut two strips to that exact measurement (which should equal 13"). Sew to the sides of the block and press the seam allowances to the border. (See also page 81.)

7. The second border consists of pieced Elies blocks. Following the directions on pages 65 to 66, construct them from the 6" and 4½" squares cut from reproduction fabric in step 2. Choose the colors carefully when you pair the squares, first for making Hourglass blocks, then when bringing the two sizes together for the final Elies blocks.

8. Make two horizontal sets of three Elies blocks by sewing together side-by-side and two vertical sets of five by sewing together end-to-end.

9. Match the horizontal rows to the top and bottom of the center block, pinning carefully in place to maintain the width of narrow border that is already in place, and to maintain sharp points in the corners of the Elies blocks. Stitch, then press seam allowances gently toward the narrow border. Repeat for the vertical borders.

10. Apply the third narrow border in the same manner as the first border (see step 6).

11. The final cream border, is 5" wide when finished and features corner blocks made from a decorative print. Construct the corner blocks simply by cutting four 5½" squares with a motif or pattern you like at the center. Fuse a second, smaller square (3⅝") on top, placing it on point.

12. Measure the quilt horizontally through the center (see page 81). Cut two lengths from the 5½" wide border strips to that measurement for the top and bottom borders. Pin the borders in place by matching the center of the border to the center of the quilt. Stitch in place.

13. Repeat Step 12, this time measuring vertically through the center of the quilt. Sew the corner squares from Step 11 to either end of each border strip, then sew the vertical borders in position.

FINISHING

14. Follow the directions on pages 50 to 51 and 90 to 91 to quilt and bind your quilt. I decided that pomegranates made a nice motif for quilting in the wide, light tan border.

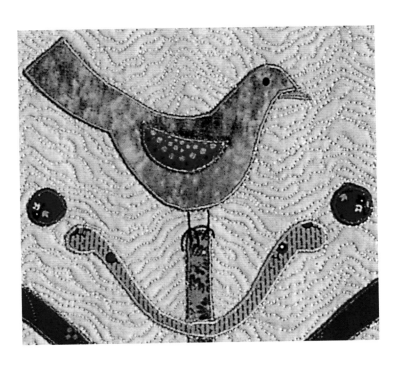

1776 Sampler

*Who could resist that pretty
checkerboard design? I certainly couldn't!*

My name, Liz Needle, is appropriate for a quilter. I'm a full-time primary school teacher and, a very much part-time quilter. I started my sampler hesitantly, but before long I was totally involved and had to be restrained from adding more and more borders. My involvement with the Retreating Angels has been the most important influence on my quilting and the inspiration for me to move beyond the parameters I had set for myself.

MATERIALS

Center checkerboard, background and border: ¼ yard white or cream fabric

Alternate squares on checkerboard and first border: ¼ yard turkey red fabric

Background of second border: ½ yard of deep teal fabric

Appliqués for third border and pomegranate border: scraps in solid color

Third border: ¼ yard of solid gold

Elies border: 1½ yards of light, medium, and dark patterned fabrics

Fifth border: ¼ yard of solid medium blue

Pomegranates border: ½ yard of black fabric for background

Backing: 1½ yards

Binding: 1 yard

Thin cotton batting: 1½ yards

Fusible web and stabilizer

Finished size: 44" x 44" plus binding

TEMPLATES

For checkerboard border, use template set A (mini-pomegranate—prepare 8); template B (dot—prepare 30); template C (diamond—prepare 4); template set H (leaf—prepare 1, prepare 1 reverse); template set J (star—prepare 3); template set G (starburst—prepare 1, omitting half moons) and template set K (starburst with circle—prepare 2) on page 139. Reduce all to fit into a background strip that finishes at 1 ½" wide (v" narrower than checkerboard border in 1776).

For tree appliqué, use template set C (cactus tree—prepare 2, prepare 2 reverse) on page 156. Reduce to fit into a border that finishes at 5" wide.

For Bautzen block, use offspring template set B (small Bautzen block—prepare 6) on page 159.

For Elies blocks, use template A (large Elies block—prepare 20) on page 142.

For pomegranate border, use templates A (pomegranate—prepare 36) and B (dot—prepare 80) on page 138.

For corner appliqué, use template set A (star—prepare 4) on page 140.

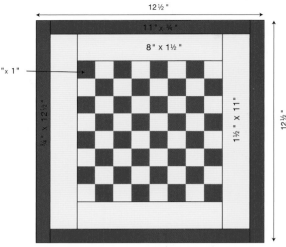

Checkerboard center

CUTTING

1. For the checkerboard, cut two 1½" wide strips, selvage to selvage, from the cream and turkey red fabrics. Cut each strip in half to make 8 strips of fabric measuring 1½" x 22."

2. For the background of the checkerboard's appliqué border, cut one 2" wide strip, selvage to selvage, from the white/cream fabric. From this strip, cut two 8½" lengths and two 11½" lengths.

3. For the solid turkey red border, cut two 1¼" wide strips, selvage to selvage, then divide into two 11½" lengths and two 13" lengths.

4. From the dark teal fabric, cut two 5½" wide strips, selvage to selvage, then divide into two 13" lengths and two 23" lengths. These will be the background for the appliqués.

5. From the solid gold fabric, cut four 1½" wide strips, selvage to selvage. From these strips, cut two lengths of 23" and two lengths of 24½".

6. For the Elies blocks, cut twenty 8" squares and twenty 6" squares.

7. From the solid medium blue fabric, cut four 1¼" wide strips, selvage to selvage. From these strips, cut two lengths of 36½" and two lengths of 38".

8. From the black fabric, cut four 4" wide strips selvage to selvage. From these strips, cut four 38" lengths and four 4" squares.

SEWING AND APPLIQUE

9. For the checkerboard, sew the red and white strips together in alternating colors to make a rectangle measuring 8½" x 22". (See also page 71.) Press all seams in the same direction. Cut eight 1½" wide strips across the width of the rectangle, and re-sew the strips together, alternating the colors to form a checkerboard block that is 8½" square. See also pages 70 to 73.

10. Attach the appliqués as shown in the photograph, following the directions for machine appliqué on pages 62 to 63 and page 67. The 8I/2" background strips are for the top and bottom bor-

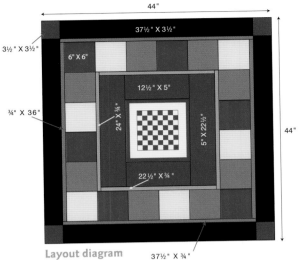

Layout diagram

44"

37½" X 3½"

3½" X 3½"

6" X 6"

12½" X 5"

¾" X 36"

24" X ¾"

5" X 22½"

44"

22½" X ¾"

37½" X ¾"

ders, and the 11½" backgrounds strips are for the side borders, with the pomegranate appliqués. Complete the appliqués, then sew the top and bottom borders onto the checkerboard, followed by the side borders.

11. For the solid turkey red border, sew the 11½" lengths to the top and bottom of the bordered checkerboard, then the 13" lengths to the sides. Stitch carefully to maintain a perfectly straight line on this border that will finish to a ¾" width.

12. For the appliqués on the wide teal border, follow step 4 on page 86 to make eight small Sorbian blocks from solid-color scraps. Assemble four Cactus Tree motifs in identical color schemes, again using solid color fabrics. Follow the directions for machine appliqué on pages 62 to 63 and page 67 to complete the appliqués. The 13" strips are for the top and bottom borders, onto which two Sorbian blocks are attached. The 23½" background strips are for the side borders. Complete the appliqué on all borders, and sew the top and bottom borders on, followed by the side borders.

13. For the solid gold borders, sew the shorter (23") lengths to the top and bottom of the center panel. Press the seam allowances toward the gold border. Then sew the side borders in place.

14. Construct 20 large Elies blocks, following the instructions on pages 65 to 66. Choose the colors carefully when you pair the 8" and 6" squares, first for the Hourglass blocks, then when bringing the two sizes together for the final Elies blocks. Arrange the completed blocks in two horizontal sets of four then sew them together side-by-side. Arrange two vertical sets of six, sewing them together end-to-end. Match the horizontal rows to the top and bottom of the center block, pinning carefully in place to maintain the width of the narrow gold border, and to maintain sharp points in the corners of the Elies blocks. Stitch, then press the seam allowances gently toward the narrow border. Repeat for the vertical borders of Elies blocks.

15. For the solid medium blue borders, sew the shorter (36½") lengths to the top and bottom of the center panel. Press the seam allowances toward the solid blue border. Then sew the side borders (38" long) in place and press all seam allowances to the solid blue border.

16. For the final appliqué border, assemble 36 pomegranate motifs from scraps of solid-color fabrics (with red center pieces), following the directions on page 75. Assemble four three-color, six-pointed, stars in different color schemes, again using solid color fabrics. Cut 80 circles from various solid color fabrics after applying fusible web to the wrong side of the fabrics. Attach the motifs to the background strips and corner squares, following the directions for machine appliqué on pages 62 to 63 and page 67. Make four identical borders, and sew the top and bottom borders in place. Sew corner squares to both ends of the two side borders, then sew them in place.

FINISHING

17. Follow the directions on pages 50 to 52 and pages 90 to 91 to quilt and bind your quilt.

The King of Eagles

My medallion-style quilt showcases the doubleheaded eagle, along with other appliqué motifs

The motif for the double-headed eagle from Pam Holland's *1776* quilt grabbed me when I first saw it, and it was a natural choice for the primary motif in my offspring quilt. I am always interested in learning what inspired a particular quilt, whether it be a new class, or nature, or special photos. I enjoy the many aspects of quilting and am always humbled at how sharing fellow patchwork enthusiasts can be and the wonderful friendships quilting builds.

MATERIALS

Backgrounds of center square and some of appliquéd border blocks, plus details on Elies blocks: ¾ yard of light-colored fabric

Narrow bands on either side of Elies blocks, plus binding: ¾ yard of rusty red fabric

Background of Elies blocks and corner squares of outside border: fat quarter of dark brown fabric

Details in Elies blocks and backgrounds in appliqué border: about ⅛ yard in variety of light fabrics

Appliqués in center block and appliqué border: about ¼ yard in variety of medium and dark fabrics

Backing: 1 yard

Binding: 1 yard

Thin cotton batting: 1 yard

Fusible web and stabilizer

Finished size: 36" x 36" plus binding

TEMPLATES

For eagle motif, use template set B on page 155 (prepare 1).

For flower, use template set F on page 137 (prepare 1, prepare 1 reverse; for flying bird, use offspring template C on page 161 (prepare 3).

For Elies block, use template set A on page 138 (prepare 20).

For corner blocks (wend), use template set L on page 139. Enlarge by 200% (prepare 4).

For star in vertical borders, use template set A on page 140. Reduce to fit on a 5 ½" wide strip (prepare 2).

For starburst, use template set I (star on star) on page 139. Reduce to fit on a 5 ½" wide strip (prepare 4).

For large and small deer, use template set P (shade tree) on page 148. Reduce slightly to fit as desired onto a 5 ½" wide strip (prepare 2 large, prepare 1 large reverse; prepare 1 small, prepare 1 small reverse).

For flower in pot, use template set A (flower tree) on page 155. Reduce to fit on a 5 ½" wide strip (prepare 1).

For cactus, use template set C (cactus tree) on page 156. Reduce to fit on a 5 ½" wide strip (prepare 1).

For bird, use template set A (partridge in a pear tree) on page 151. Enlarge to fit on a 5 ½" wide strip (prepare 1, prepare 1 reverse).

For star in bottom border, use template set T (star and balloons) on page 150. Reduce to fit on a 5 ½" wide strip (prepare 2).

For butterfly, use template set D (butterfly 1) on page 140, omiting some of the dots (prepare 1).

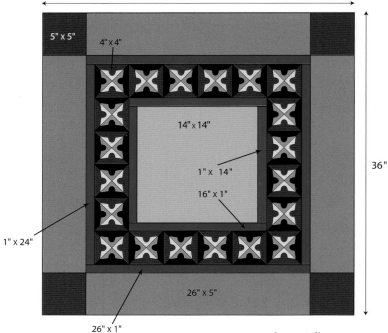

Layout diagram

CUTTING

1. From the light-colored fabric, cut a 15½" square for the background of the center block and a 5½" wide strip across the width of the fabric to be used as desired as background for the appliquéd blocks of the outer border.

2. From the rusty red fabric, cut six 1½" wide strips for the narrow bands on either side of the Elies blocks.

3. From the dark brown fabric, cut twenty 6" squares for the background of the Elies blocks and four 5½" squares for the corner blocks of the appliqué border.

4. From the variety of light-colored fabrics, cut 5½" wide strips in random lengths to make squares or rectangles. Study the photograph to see how these strips are used as background for the appliqué blocks of the outer border. Cut four 3" squares for the corner blocks insets.

SEWING AND APPLIQUÉ

5. For the center square, use the templates listed above, reducing and enlarging as directed to make the appliqué patterns. Assemble and apply the motifs to the background square, following the directions for machine appliqué on pages 62 to 63 and page 67. When appliqué is complete, trim the center block back to precisely 14½" square.

6. Use two of the rusty red 1½" wide strips to make the first border around the center square. Cut a 15" length and a 17" length from each strip; sew the shorter ones to either side; press the seam allowances gently toward the border. Sew the longer strips to the top and bottom of the center square and press the seam allowances toward the border.

7. The Elies block in this quilt is a modification of the original, in that the background is not a pieced hourglass block. It is a solid 6" dark brown square. Follow steps 7 to 10 on page 66 to attach the four-petal center shape to the squares (rather than to the Hourglass blocks in the original quilt). To aid in positioning the four-petal shape, fold the background square in half on the diagonal and lightly press along the fold; repeat for the opposite direction. You will have an X pressed into the background square to guide you in correctly placing the seams of the four-petal shape.

8. When all 20 Elies blocks are complete, make two vertical strips of four blocks by sewing them together end-to-end and two horizontal rows of six by sewing together side-by-side. Match the vertical rows to the sides of the center square, pinning carefully in place to maintain the width of the narrow rust-red border. Stitch, then press seam allowances gently toward the border. Repeat for the horizontal rows of Elies blocks.

9. For the next round of borders, use the four remaining 1½" wide rusty red strips. Measure vertically through the middle of the center block and cut two strips to that length. Carefully match the center of the strip to the center of the Elies border, and aligning ends; pin in place. Stitch, carefully maintaining a constant seam allowance. Press the seam allowances toward the border. Repeat for the top and bottom borders.

10. For the final appliquéd border, make the background by randomly stitching together the 5½" wide squares or rectangles of different light-colored fabrics. Determine the length by measuring through the center of the quilt. Cut four pieced strips to equal that length. Using the photograph as a guide, prepare, assemble, and attach the motifs, following the directions for machine appliqué on pages 62 to 63 and page 67.

11. Appliqué the four corner blocks. Stitch one to either end of each horizontal strip. Apply the vertical appliquéd borders to the sides of the center square, then sew the horizontal borders/corner blocks to the top and bottom.

FINISHING

12. Follow the directions on pages 50 to 52 and 90 to 91 to quilt and bind your quilt. I decided that pomegranates made a nice motif for quilting in the cream-colored border.

The Four Horsemen

The soldiers on horseback brandishing swords were my favorite motifs

The moment Pam Holland invited me to make quilt using the patterns from *1776*, I immediately decided on my favorite color, purple, as a background. Like the center block of Pam's quilt, I wanted a star to be the focus of attention. I added extra star points to make it even more striking. I thought Elies blocks—in bright colors--would look great as a border around the star. I put the star on point, allowing the soldiers on horseback to chase each other around the quilt. Before sewing on the borders, I added a flange to give the small-block border greater definition.

Since Pam and I share a similar family heritage, this project held an unusual fascination for me. *The Four Horsemen* will always have special meaning.

MATERIALS

Background and corner triangles: I yard dark-colored fabric (I chose a mottled purple that gives the appearance of a hand-dyed fabric)

Elies blocks and border squares: 6 fat quarters in different bright solid colors

Center star and narrow flange next to border of squares: ¾ yard yellow fabric

Rays of star: fat eighth each of gold and pumpkin fabric

Horses: fat eighth each of grey and brown fabric

Details on soldier's and horses uniforms: assorted scraps or fat eighths of solid-color fabrics

Gold metallic thread

Backing: 1¼ yard

Binding and hanging sleeve: I yard

Thin cotton batting: 1¼ yard

Fusible web and fabric stabilizer

Finished size: 37 ½" x 37 ½" plus binding

TEMPLATES

For center circle, use template D (from center square) on page 137.

For longest star point, use template B (from Center Square) on page 136. Do not add seam allowance (prepare 4).

For medium star point, use template C (from Center Square) on page 136. Do not add seam allowance (prepare 4).

For short star point, use offspring template D (short star point) on page 159. Do not add seam allowance (prepare 4).

For Elies blocks, use template A (small Elies block) on page 138 (prepare 21).

For cavalryman, use template set C (from Date Panel) on page 153. Enlarge to fill background triangles (prepare 4).

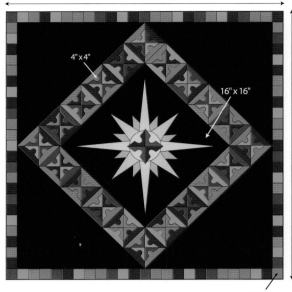

Layout diagram

CUTTING

1. For the background, cut a 17½" square of the dark mottled blue fabric for the center.

2. For the corner triangles, cut two 19¾" squares. Cut each square diagonally through the center to make four half-square triangles. If you wish, cut your square larger, then trim your triangles back when sewing them in place in step 9.

3. For the Elies blocks, cut twenty 6" squares and twenty-one 4½" squares from the fat quarters of bright colors.

4. For the outer border, cut eighty-six 2" squares from the same bright colors.

5. For the narrow yellow border, which is actually a three-dimensional flange, cut four 1¼" wide strips across the width of the yellow fabric.

SEWING AND APPLIQUÉ

6. For the star motif, use the templates listed above and follow the directions for machine appliqué on pages 62 to 63 and page 67 to make the appliqué pieces. Group the four long star points and the center circle together, the medium size points together, and the small points together as you trace them onto the fusible web. Cut the groups apart and iron the first group onto the wrong side of the yellow fabric, the second group to the wrong side of the gold fabric, and the third group to the wrong side of the pumpkin fabric. Follow the directions for machine appliqué on pages 62to 63 to add first the short, then the medium, then the long star points to the background square. Embroider in place as directed on page 67. Trim the center square to 16½".

7. Construct 21 small Elies blocks, following the instructions on pages 65 to 66. Using gold metallic thread, run an extra line of stiches from each star point out to the edge of the center square. Before fusing the last block, discard the hourglass background. Fuse the four-petaled motif only to the center of the star from step 5 and embroider in place. With the remaining twenty Elies blocks, make two horizontal sets of four by sewing together side-by-side and two vertical sets of six by sewing together end-to-end. Pin the horizontal rows to the top and bot-

tom of the large star square, carefully matching mid-points and aligning ends. Stitch in place, and gently press the seam allowances toward the center block. Pin the vertical rows to either side of the large star square, again matching mid-points and aligning the ends. Stitch in place and press the seam allowances toward the center square.

8. Following the directions for machine appliqué on pages 62 to 63 and page 67, assemble the appliqués of the cavalrymen on a craft mat and embroider them to the corner triangles as shown.

9. Right sides together, pin the long edge of the first corner triangle to one side of the center square, handling carefully to avoid stretching this bias edge. Match mid-points and allow the ends of the triangle to extend slightly beyond the corners of the center square. Stitch in place, then repeat the process on the opposite side of the square. Add the two remaining corner triangles, pressing the seam allowances toward the triangles.

10. A flange is a three-dimensional detail that adds a splash of color to a quilt, just as a border would. To construct it, simply trim the four strips of yellow fabric to match the length of the quilt as measured either horizontally or vertically through the center. (Because the quilt is a square, the measurement should be the same in both directions.) Fold the strip in half lengthwise, wrong sides together, and place it on the quilt with raw edges aligned. Stitch with a ¼" seam, and press the flange flat over the quilt. Begin with one side, then do the opposite side, and finally the last two sides.

11. For the final border, stitch two strips of twenty-three 2" squares and two strips of twenty-five 2" squares, placing the colors randomly or in any sequence you wish. Sew the two shorter strips on opposite sides of the quilt and the longer strips on the two remaining sides.

FINISHING THE QUILT

12. Follow the directions on pages 50 to 51 and pages 90 to 91 to quilt and bind your quilt.

Elvira Richardson

Soldiers' Stories

Cavalry and infantrymen march around the blocks

The motifs from *1776* that most appealed to me were the soldiers. I decided to make a quilt that could become a gift for my grandsons, as they, like most small boys, are fascinated by stories of soldiers and battles from any era. I like to think they will make up their own stories about the soldiers and what they are doing.

Materials

Four blocks and the outer border: 1 yard of a light-colored fabric

Center and four corner blocks: ⅝ yard of a dark-colored fabric

First border and binding: 1 yard of a different dark-colored fabric

Soldiers, animals, and stars: fat eighths or scraps in an assortment of colors

Backing: 1½ yard

Binding: 1½ yards

Thin cotton batting: 1½ yard

Fusible web and stabilizer

Finished size: 38" x 38" plus binding

TEMPLATES

For animals, use template D (bottom jumping dog) and template E (top jumping dog) on page 144 (prepare 2 each, plus 2 reverse each); and template P (shade tree—larger deer only) on page 148 (prepare 4, prepare 4 reverse). Enlarge each template as necessary to fill a 4 ½" wide border.

For corner stars, use template set A (star) on page 140 (prepare 4).

For soldiers at center, use template set D (soldier with pipe) on page 155 (prepare 4). Reduce to fill a 8" square when placed on diagonal.

For infantrymen, use template set B (infantryman) on page 152 (prepare 4). Reduce to fill a 10" square.

For the cavalrymen, use template set C (cavalryman) on page 153 (prepare 4). Enlarge to nicely fill an 8" x 10" rectangle.

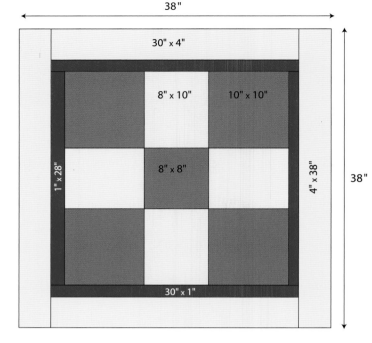

Layout diagram

CUTTING

1. For the wide outer border, cut four 4½" wide strips across the width of the light-colored fabric.

2. For the background blocks, cut four 8½" x 10½" rectangles from the light fabric, four 10½" squares from the dark fabric, and one 8½" square in the dark fabric.

3. For the narrow first border, cut four 1½" wide strips across the width of the fabric. Cut the remainder into 3" wide strips for the binding.

SEWING AND APPLIQUÉING

4. For the appliqués on the field of the quilt, use the templates listed above and follow the directions on pages 62 to 63 and page 67 to make the appliqué motifs. Assemble and apply each motif to its correct background square or rectangle. Refer to the photograph to determine correct placement of motifs. To aid in placing the four pipe-smoking soldiers of the center square, lightly draw two diagonal lines from corner to corner across the square to act as mid-points for centering each motif in its corner.

5. When the nine blocks of the center of the quilt have been appliquéd and embroidered, set them together as shown in the photograph.

6. To make the narrow first border, trim two of the 1½" wide strips to equal the length of the quilt as measured through the center in either direction (see page 81). Pin the border to quilt, carefully matching mid-points and aligning ends. Stitch in place, and gently press the seam allowance toward the border. Repeat for the opposite side. Measure the quilt across the center again, including the two borders. It should measure 2½" longer than the first measurement. Trim the two remaining border strips to this length and sew in place as directed above.

7. Follow the same procedure of measuring and trimming to fit to apply the wide outer border strips in the light fabric. Press the seam allowances toward the narrow border. Appliqué the motifs in place only after the borders have been attached to the quilt, so that you might work out the best placement of the motifs.

FINISHING

8. Follow the directions on pages 50 to 51 and pages 90 to 91 to quilt and bind your quilt.

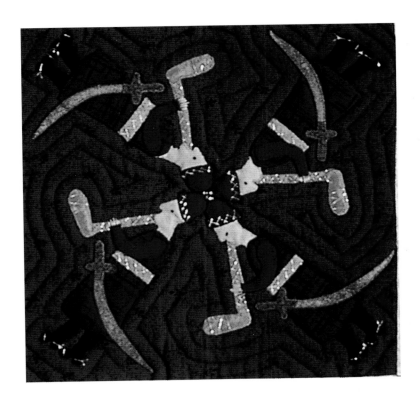

Claire's Way

Pretty pots of flowers
anchor each corner of the quilt

The Elies and Notch blocks are so unusual and distinctive that I wanted to feature them in my quilt. I decided to combine them into borders around the center block. The arrangement I chose creates the impression of an on-point square surrounding the center motif. I also enjoyed Pam Holland's flower pot design was used as an anchor in each corner of my rectangular quilt.

MATERIALS

Background of center square: fat quarter of cream-colored fabric

Background of corner blocks: ¼ yard (or fat quarter) of dark fabric

Pieced blocks and appliqué: 15 fat eighths of light and dark colors of reproduction fabrics

Narrow inside border: ¼ yard solid dark blue fabric

Outside border and binding: 1 yard rusty red fabric

Backing: 1 yard

Binding: 1 yard

Batting: 1 yard

Fusible web and stabilizer

Finished size: 32 ½" x 39 ½" plus binding

TEMPLATES

For Elies blocks, use template A (small Elies block) on page 138 (prepare 12).

For Notch blocks, use template A (Notch block) on page 138 (prepare 6).

For corner flowers, use template set A (flower tree) on page 155 (prepare 4 reverse sets). For center, use template set C (cactus tree) on page 156 (prepare 1). Enlarge to fill an 8" square.

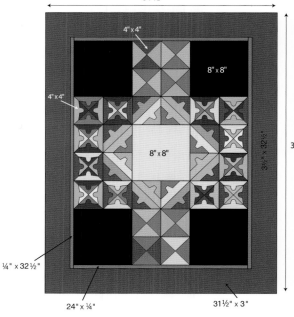

Layout diagram

CUTTING

1. From the cream-colored fabric, cut a 9" square. From the dark fabric, cut four 9" squares.

2. From the fat eighths of reproduction fabric, cut twelve 6" squares, twenty 4" squares, and sixteen 5" squares.

3. From the solid dark blue fabric, cut four ¾" wide strips across the width of the fabric.

4. From the rusty red fabric, cut four 4" wide strips across the width of the fabric for the border. Cut the remainder into 3" wide strips for the binding.

SEWING AND APPLIQUÉING

5. For the center and four corner appliqué blocks, use the templates listed above and follow the directions for machine appliqué on pages 62 to 63 and page 67 to assemble, make, fuse, and embroider around the appliqué motifs. Note that the cactus tree motif goes on the light background, and the four flowering trees go on the dark backgrounds. Mix up the fabrics for the flowers on the trees—the quilt is more interesting if these four motifs are not identical. Trim the five appliquéd blocks back to a precise 8½" square.

6. Follow the directions on pages 65 to 66 to make up twelve small Elies blocks, using all of the 6" squares and twelve of the 4" squares that you cut. Choose the colors carefully when you pair the squares, first for the Hourglass blocks, then when bringing the two sizes together for the finished Elies blocks.

7. Follow the directions on pages 68 to 69 to make up eight 4" Notch blocks, using eight of the 5" squares you cut and the eight remaining 4" squares. Again, choose colors carefully in all steps of construction.

8. Sew the Notch blocks together in pairs, paying attention to the photograph to determine the best layout. Sew a pair to the top of the center square and another pair to the bottom of the center square. Again using the photograph as a guide, sew an Elies block to both ends of both remaining pairs. Sew on these two vertical sets. Complete the center section by sewing two sections of four Elies blocks together end-to-end and attaching them to the two sides of the panel.

9. Using the eight remaining 5" squares, make eight 4" Hourglass blocks, following steps 1 to 5 on pages 65 to 66. Notice that each Hourglass block in the quilt has a set of blue triangles. You may

wish to plan a similar color scheme, or choose a completely different one. Just make sure that you begin each set of Hourglass blocks with a pair of squares that are high in contrast—one light and one dark.

10. Sew the Hourglass squares into two sets of four blocks. Sew an appliquéd flower tree block to each side of the two sets of Hourglass blocks. Attach a completed row to the top of the center panel and the other to the bottom.

11. To make the narrow dark blue border, trim two of the ¾" wide strips to equal the length of the quilt taken vertically through the center (see page 81). Pin the border to the side of the quilt, carefully matching mid-points and aligning ends and edges. Stitch in place, taking care to maintain an even ¼" seam allowance. Gently press the seam allowance toward the border. Repeat for the opposite side. Measure the quilt horizontally across the center, including the two borders. Trim the two remaining border strips to this length and sew to the top and bottom of the quilt as directed above.

12. Follow the same procedure of measuring and trimming to fit to apply the wide outer border strips in the rusty red fabric. Press the seam allowances toward the red border.

FINISHING

13. Follow the directions on pages 50 to 51 and pages 90 to 91 to quilt and bind your quilt.

Afterword

1776 Comes Full Circle

All my hopes and none of my fears are realized, as 1776 goes on show

1776 on Show

During June, July, and August of 2003, I was booked to tour and teach across the United States, and I decided to take *1776* with me. I had entered it in the Minnesota Quilt Show, a venue in which I'd had success with earlier quilts.

After twenty-four hours of travel, I arrived in Minnesota in the wee hours of the morning to hand the quilt over for judging. Upon opening one of my bags, I discovered half the contents were missing! Quilts, books for gifts, my electrical goods and papers—all gone! *1776* was in another bag and my heart was in my throat as I opened it. To my immense relief, it was still there.

But what of the missing quilts? Sick to my stomach, I kept asking myself, "Who would do such a thing?" as I desperately tried to convince the airline of the value of my loss. My pleas fell on deaf ears, and, rather than obtaining any real help, I was instead treated merely as an irate passenger. Little did they know what went into the making of those three lost quilts.

I did not attend the official opening of the quilt show the next evening, preferring to share quiet time at the hotel with my friend Joan Dougherty, who was also attending the show. I had signed up for some classes, and looked forward to being a student for a few days. Imagine my surprise when I walked into my first class to a standing ovation! Only then did I learn that *1776* had won Best of Show!

It is very difficult, when you work on a project for as long as I worked on *1776*, to have a sense of how good the quilt really is. I must confess that the comment "It's only a copy," from my Aussie quilting colleague had needled me, and I wanted other opinions. With the naming of this quilt—my eight-year obsession—as Best of Show, it was as if all the work I had done came back to embrace me.

I continued my teaching tour through the United States with the quilt at my side. Of course, I never transported it in my luggage again. In fact, it now travels with me as hand luggage in a large bag and never leaves my sight.

By mid-journey, in July of 2003, I decided to take a nine-day break with my friend Lisa Blevins. We hired a silver Pontiac TransAm, had our nails done (complete with small rhinestones on our pinkie fingers), then packed our clothes, Diet Coke®, a pistol, and off we went. We didn't know exactly where we were going, just in the direction of the Grand Canyon and Las Vegas.

We stopped at every quilt shop along the way. We talked non-stop, solved the world's and everyone else's problems, and listened to loud country music. We dressed in shorts and tee shirts. It was just fabulous. Lisa's high-pressure job and my busy schedule were left behind.

In Sedona, Arizona, we came across the Quilters' Store and Gallery. We visited for a short time, and then my accent was commented on by one of the women behind the counter. Lisa, in her effervescent manner, gave my full history in the span of thirty seconds, then punctuated it by saying, "You should see what we have in the trunk!" We brought *1776* out for viewing, and I told its story. The proprietor, Marge Elson, happened to be there. "You have to take this quilt up to 'Quilt Camp in the Pines' at Flagstaff. They would love to see it," she urged us.

Several hours later, Lisa and I, still in our traveling clothes, arrived at Northern Arizona University in Flagstaff where the annual Quilting Camp was being held. We walked sheepishly up to the reception desk and said, "We've been asked to bring this quilt to show you." The efficient girl on the desk said, "Oh, Show-and-Tell is not until tonight, so bring it back at 7:30." Lisa and I made a quick trip to the Grand Canyon, raced to the rim, took copious amounts of photos, and arrived back at the University just in time to catch the last part of Show-and-Tell. I registered that I had a quilt to share and was told to go to the end of the line.

After everyone else had proudly shown their projects, I was introduced and brought out my 1776 quilt. I was overwhelmed at the reaction. The room descended upon me, and I spent a long time answering questions.

Lisa and I parted company in early August after a wonderful time in Las Vegas. I had my mind on the "Quilt Odyssey" show in Gettysburg, Pennsylvania, which began on July 31, 2003. We had shipped *1776* to Gettysburg while in Las Vegas, and I was nervous to know that it had arrived safely. Imagine how I felt when I learned that, not only had it arrived, it had won another Best of Show award! I was thrilled—elated. It was another outstanding affirmation of the quality of the quilt.

I returned home to continue teaching, leaving the quilt in the care of Joan Dougherty to be sent to Houston. After having those quilts stolen from my luggage, I was very nervous about leaving the quilt, let alone shipping it. However, I finally put everything in perspective: it is, after all, just a quilt.

Keith and I made plans to attend Quilt Market and Festival; it was going to a special time for us. We planned to take a three-week holiday and travel after the event.

On the evening of October 20, I said goodbye to two of our children, Jamie and Rachael. We sat in the dining room and had coffee, talked of recent events, and shared my excitement about the forthcoming trip. Ten minutes after the children left, a breathless Keith called to say that our son Matthew and his partner Karen had been involved in an accident not far from our home.

I don't think I will ever forget the tears in Keith's voice as we raced to the hospital. I decided right away that I must cancel my trip and stay with my family. Matthew's side was completely crushed, having taken the blow when the other car rammed his broadside. His leg was broken in many places, his arm was crushed, and nerves were severed. Karen died some hours after reaching the hospital, and our world fell apart.

Sorbs in America

Another chapter in the story of *1776* revealed itself during the International Quilt Festival in Houston. When not in class, I spent as much time as possible next to the quilt. I chatted to hundreds of people, many of them men fascinated that the original quilt had been made by soldiers. Upon publication of an article in *The Houston Chronicle*, I immediately began receiving phone calls from people who, although not quilters, had a cultural connection to the Sorbs (also known as Wends). As it turns out, in mid-1854 a tall-masted ship named the Ben Nevis had landed in Galveston, carrying Sorbian (Wendish) immigrants seeking a place where they could practice their religion in freedom. Five hundred eighty-eight men, women, and children began the voyage, but 78 died from cholera during the crossing. The 510 who lived made the long trek inland to Houston by oxcart and on foot. Although many of them were struck down by the yellow fever epidemic of the time, the survivors struggled through bleak winters and hot dry summers to establish the Texas town of Serbin,

After reading about the quilt in the news-paper, a good-hearted pastor named Mr. Walter Dube contacted us with news about Serbin. Later he brought his family for a delightful and informative dinner visit, during which he told Keith and me the history of the little town. We became convinced that it was important to visit there, and, since we had the luxury of a rental car, we took off to find it. I rejoiced in the town's museum, which was filled with memorabilia that reminded me of my own family's flight from Bautzen to Australia, and, of course, of the connection to the quilt. It was such a coincidence to be in America, yet to be so close to my own cultural heritage, a unique combination of Sorb (Wend) and Australian.

Published in The Illustrated London News *in 1852, this etching is labeled "The New Australian Emigrant Packet-Ship, Ben Nevis"*

Despite my decision to the contrary, the family insisted that I go to Houston. Vainly I reiterated my commitment to staying with them; as a group, they insisted I maintain my schedule. So it was that, drugged on tranquilizers and cared for by Qantas Airlines, I made a very dazed plane trip across the ocean. Meantime, and without my knowledge, Keith called the management at Quilt Festival and explained my situation. Consequently, when I arrived I found the show staff to be marvelously solicitous. In addition to their support, my friend Joan Dougherty had flown down from Minnesota especially to be with me. I would never have made it through that emotional time without them.

The day of the announcement of the quilt show winners arrived, and was also the day of Karen's funeral. I felt I had done the wrong thing in going to Houston; my heart was breaking for those at home. In an effort to cheer me up, Joan took me for a walk in the sun, and we fed the ducks in a nearby Japanese garden. In spite of the cloud of sorrow surrounding me, I finally began nervously to anticipate the upcoming events.

Time for the official reception arrived, and dressed in our finery, Joan and I became caught up in the excitement of being elbow-to-elbow with television quilting celebrities like Alex Anderson and John Flynn. My nervousness and sadness started dissipating, and I began to quietly enjoy myself.

The ceremony was held in a huge ballroom, with the award-winning quilts hung high on the circular walls and shrouded by black curtains. Excitement mounted as, one by one, the curtains were raised on seventy-eight winning quilts. Finally we were down to the last six. As each award was announced, my heart beat faster and faster, while the countdown seemed to get slower and slower. Joan whispered, "Get a grip on yourself!" Finally, the last two quilts were hanging there. When the next quilt was announced, I realized that I had won America's top prize for quilts!

The room erupted—I heard my Aussie friends cheering me as I was propelled to the front of the room. From that moment on, everything was a blur. People surrounded me—I must have talked to hundreds of folks. As the crowd began to thin, I tried to call Keith, but I had to leave a message rather than talk directly with him. Finally, laden with an oversize check (five feet long by two feet wide) and a huge bunch of flowers, I caught the shuttle bus with my friends, and we went back to the hotel for a celebratory dinner and a bottle of champagne. A few days later, my dear husband flew to Houston so that we could spend a week of recovery and celebration time together.

Excitement Continues

I am a true believer in telling others of my passion. *1776* is precious to me, but I enjoy sharing it with all who are interested. It has traveled the world many times, been admired by thousands of people, and I've fished it out of the trunk of the car and shown it to the casual inquirer. I even hung it in a county fair in Perham, Minnesota, for a day!

On a more formal basis, I exhibited *1776* at the American Quilter's Society show in Nashville in August 2004, where it won Best of Show in the category of Large Wall Quilts. To my surprise, that automatically meant that it went into the 2005 AQS show in Paducah.

I think I was even more nervous at the AQS awards ceremony than I had been at Houston months earlier. I began feeling my tension level rise as I listened to Ricky Timms' entertaining opening act; it went higher as each award was presented, one by one. As the excitement grew, I vowed I would never put myself through this kind of suspense again. Finally, the announcement came that *1776* had again taken first place in its category! The audience was most generous with its support and applause, and I once more had the feeling that all those hours of work had been worth it.

Except for the time it has been on exhibit, the quilt has traveled everywhere I have gone throughout 2005 and 2006. After its time in Paducah, *1776* was shown in New Zealand at the 2005 Quilt Symposium, and later at the Australasian Quilt Festival in Melbourne.

My dream is to one day take my *1776* to Bautzen and exhibit it with the original *1776* in some kind of special venue.

What will happen to the quilt now? I do not know, exactly, but I do know that it is a continuing passion. Its effect has spread like a ripple on a pond, and it has changed my life. I have told its story hundreds of times, and I never tire of it—although I cannot explain exactly why, I believe that that I *must* share the story. Neither can I explain why folks get so emotional upon seeing the quilt, even before they hear the story. My only explanation is that this quilt, made so many years ago by unknown soldiers, was meant to be re-born, and I was selected by fate to be the one to shepherd it into its second life.

Templates

CENTER SQUARE

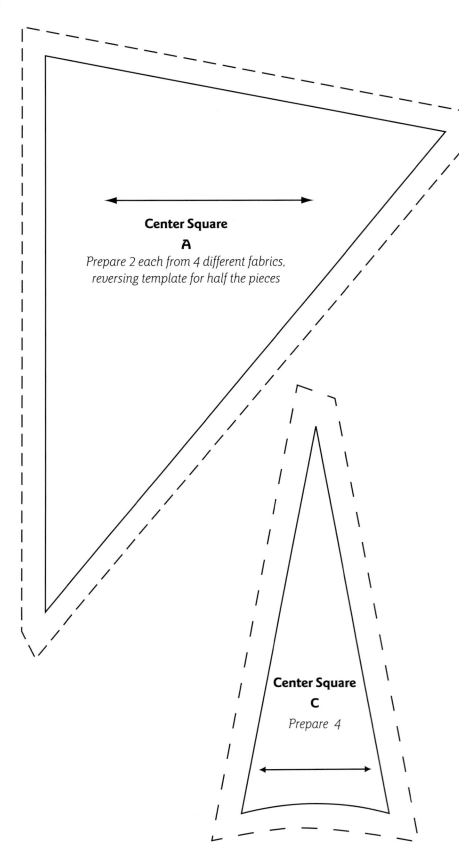

Center Square
A

*Prepare 2 each from 4 different fabrics,
reversing template for half the pieces*

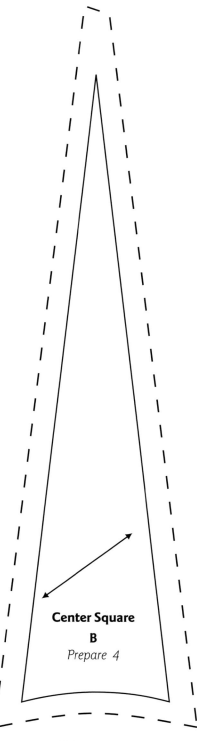

Center Square
B
Prepare 4

Center Square
C

Prepare 4

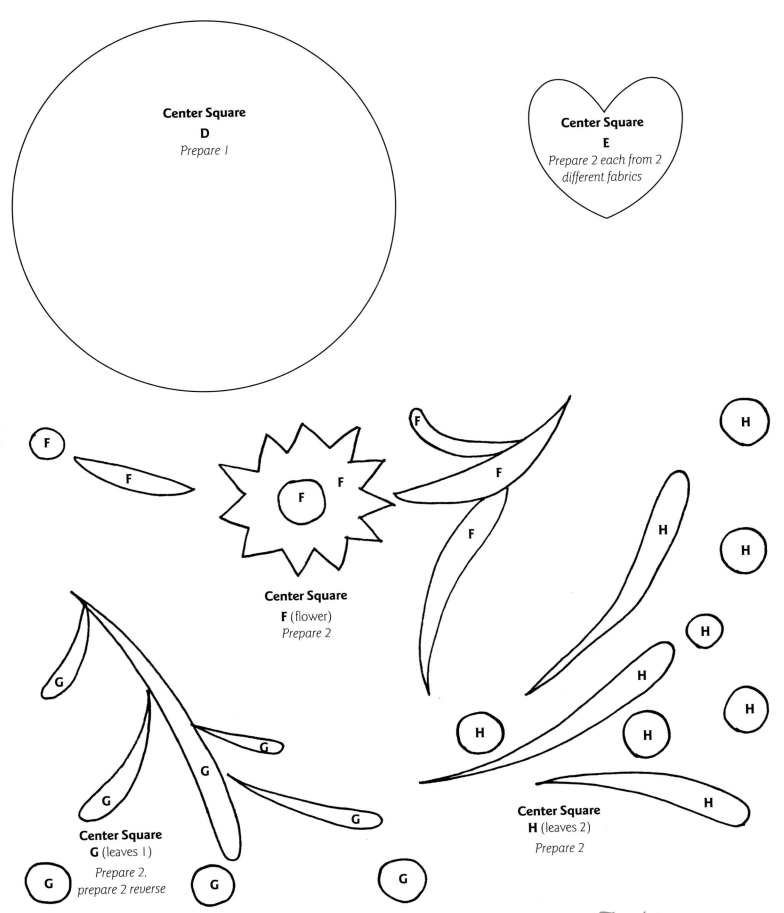

Center Square
D
Prepare 1

Center Square
E
Prepare 2 each from 2 different fabrics

Center Square
F (flower)
Prepare 2

Center Square
G (leaves 1)
Prepare 2, prepare 2 reverse

Center Square
H (leaves 2)
Prepare 2

NOTCH BLOCK

ELIES BLOCK

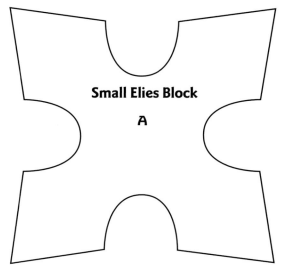

Small Elies Block

A

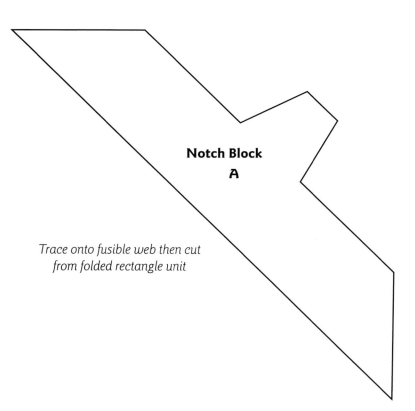

Notch Block

A

*Trace onto fusible web then cut
from folded rectangle unit*

*Trace onto fusible web then cut four-petal
shape from 4½" Hourglass blocks*

POMEGRANATE SIDE PANEL

B

Pomegranate Side Panel
B (dot)

*Prepare 48
(For outer Pomegranate Border, prepare 196)*

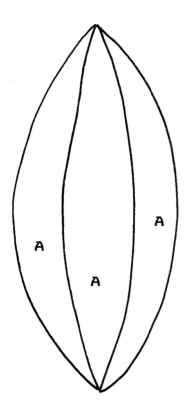

A **A**

A

Pomegranate Side Panel
A (pomegranate)

*Prepare 26
(for outer Pomegranate Border, prepare 94)*

CHECKERBOARD BORDER

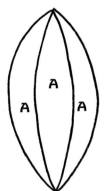

Checkerboard Border
A (mini-pomegranate)
Prepare 32

Checkerboard Border
B (small dot)
Prepare 80

Checkerboard Border
C
(diamond) Prepare 8

Checkerboard Border
D (dot)
Prepare 4

Checkerboard Border
F (small star)
Prepare 40

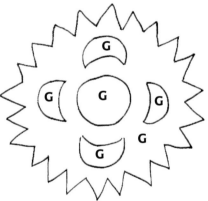

Checkerboard Border
K (starburst with circle)
Prepare 4

Checkerboard border
E (heart)
Prepare 4

Checkerboard Border
H (leaf)
Prepare 4, prepare 4 reverse

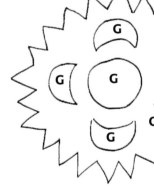

Checkerboard Border
G (starburst)
Prepare 6

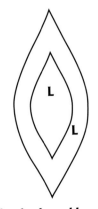

Checkerboard border
L (wend)
Prepare 8

Checkerboard border
I (star-on-star)
Prepare 2

Checkerboard border
J (star)
Prepare 2

HORIZONTAL APPLIQUÉ PANEL

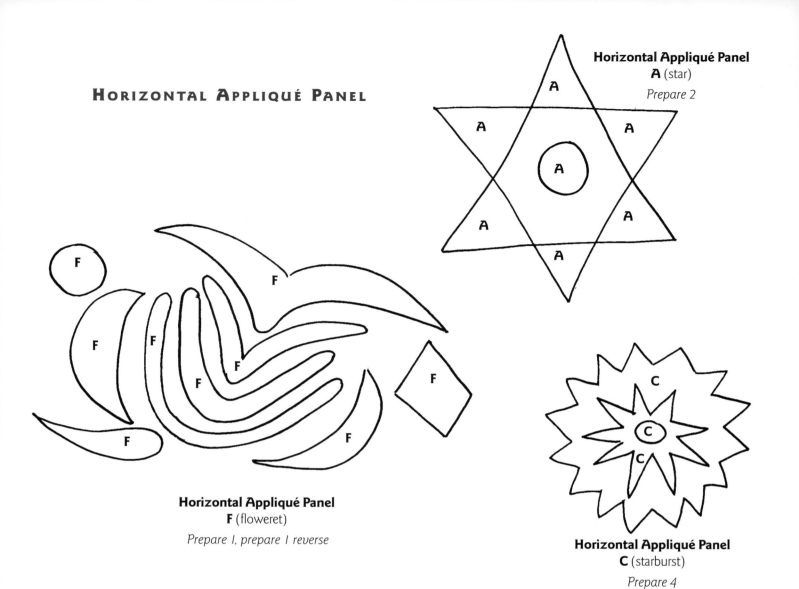

Horizontal Appliqué Panel
A (star)

Prepare 2

Horizontal Appliqué Panel
F (floweret)

Prepare 1, prepare 1 reverse

Horizontal Appliqué Panel
C (starburst)

Prepare 4

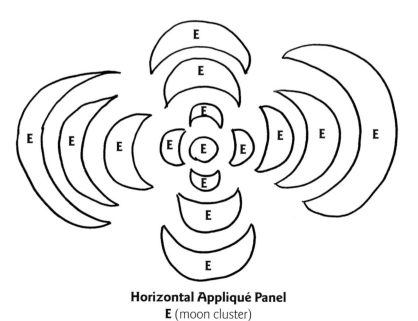

Horizontal Appliqué Panel
E (moon cluster)

Prepare 2

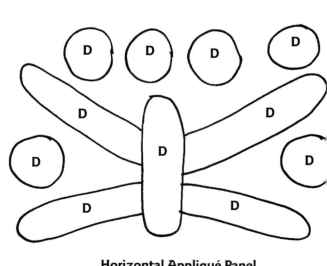

Horizontal Appliqué Panel
D (butterfly 1)

Prepare 2

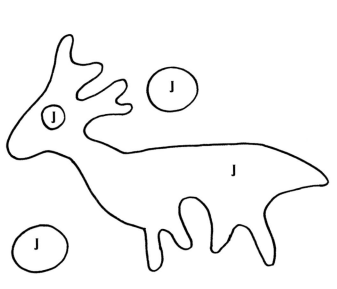

Horizontal Appliqué Panel
J (deer)

Prepare I, prepare I reverse

Horizontal Appliqué Panel
H (moon)

Prepare I, prepare I reverse

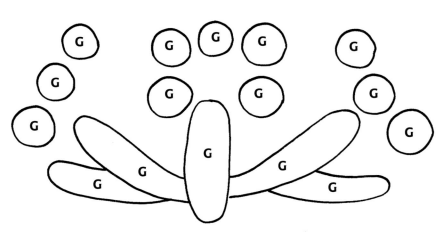

Horizontal Appliqué Panel
G (butterfly 2)

Prepare I

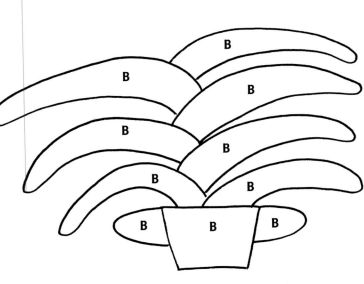

Horizontal Appliqué Panel
B (potted plant)

Prepare 5

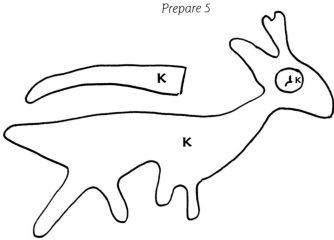

Horizontal Appliqué Panel
K (doe)

Prepare I, prepare I reverse

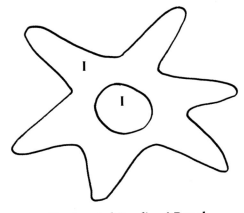

Horizontal Appliqué Panel
I (freeform star)

Prepare 4

LARGE ELIES BLOCK

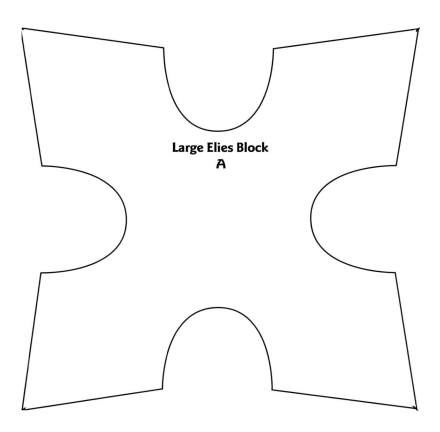

**Large Elies Block
A**

Trace onto fusible web then cut from 6" Hourglass blocks

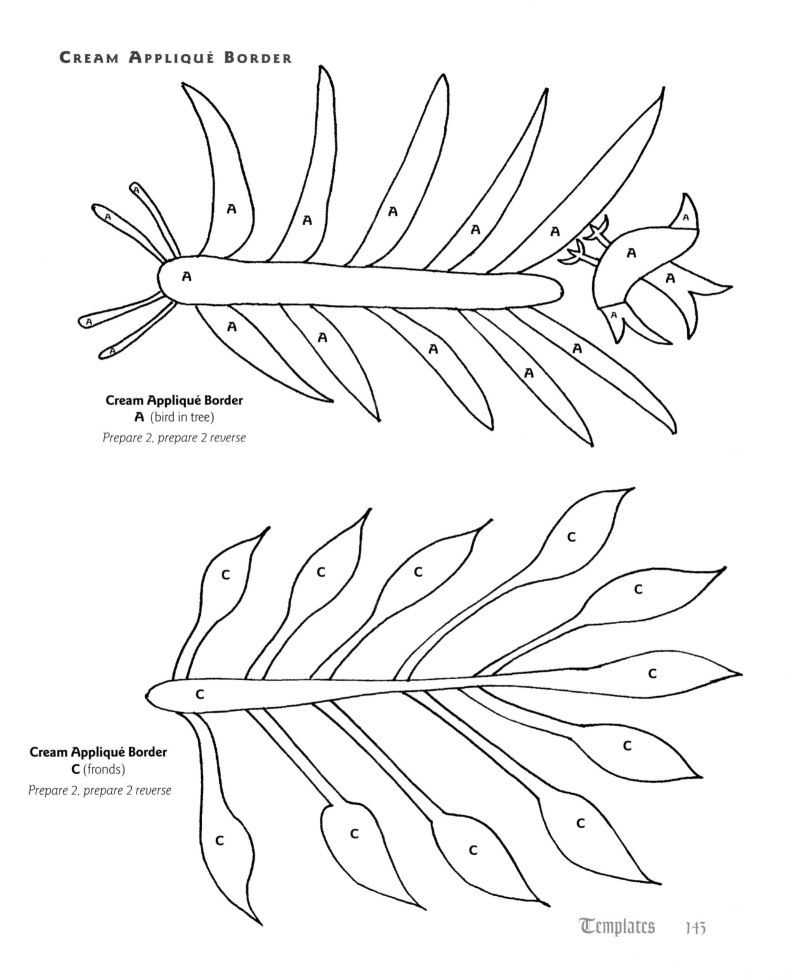

CREAM APPLIQUÉ BORDER

Cream Appliqué Border
A (bird in tree)

Prepare 2, prepare 2 reverse

Cream Appliqué Border
C (fronds)

Prepare 2, prepare 2 reverse

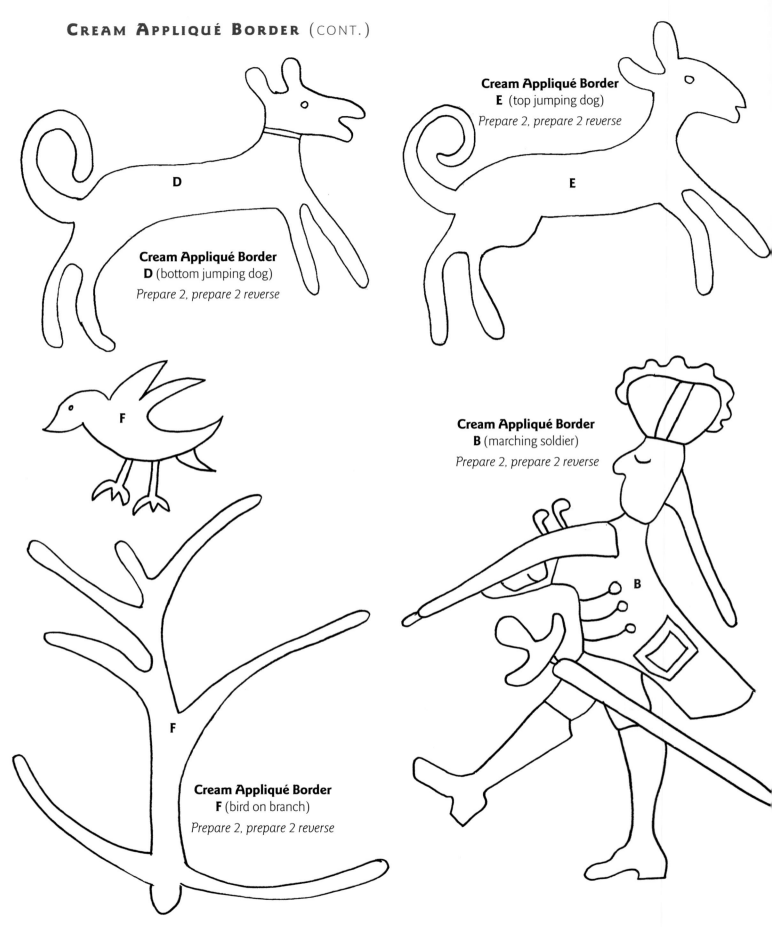

Cream Appliqué Border
E (top jumping dog)
Prepare 2, prepare 2 reverse

Cream Appliqué Border
D (bottom jumping dog)
Prepare 2, prepare 2 reverse

Cream Appliqué Border
B (marching soldier)
Prepare 2, prepare 2 reverse

Cream Appliqué Border
F (bird on branch)
Prepare 2, prepare 2 reverse

Cream Appliqué Border
I (rabbit)

Prepare 2, prepare 2 reverse

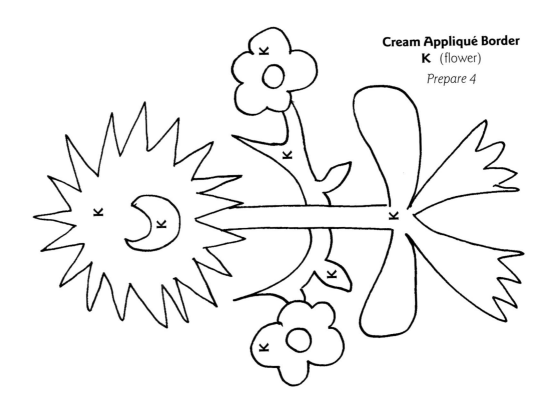

Cream Appliqué Border
K (flower)

Prepare 4

Cream Appliqué Border

N (three stars)

Prepare 2

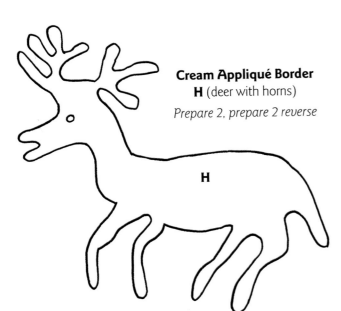

Cream Appliqué Border
H (deer with horns)

Prepare 2, prepare 2 reverse

Cream Appliqué Border
G (boar)

Prepare 2, prepare 2 reverse

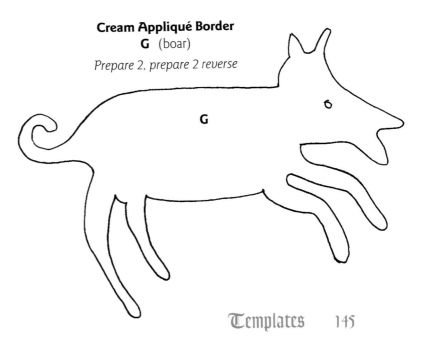

Cream Appliqué Border
J (musician)
Prepare 2, prepare 2 reverse

Cream Appliqué Border
M (starburst and balloons)
Prepare 2, prepare 2 reverse

L (balloon tree)
Prepare 2

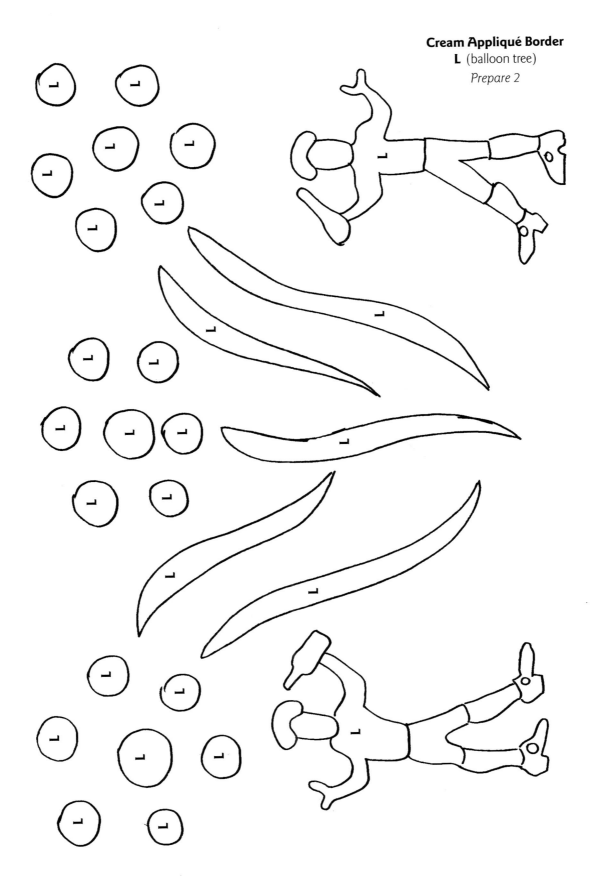

Cream Appliqué Border
U (three diamonds)
Prepare 2

Cream Appliqué Border
O (compass)
Prepare 2

Cream Appliqué Border
P (shade tree)
Prepare 1, prepare 1 reverse

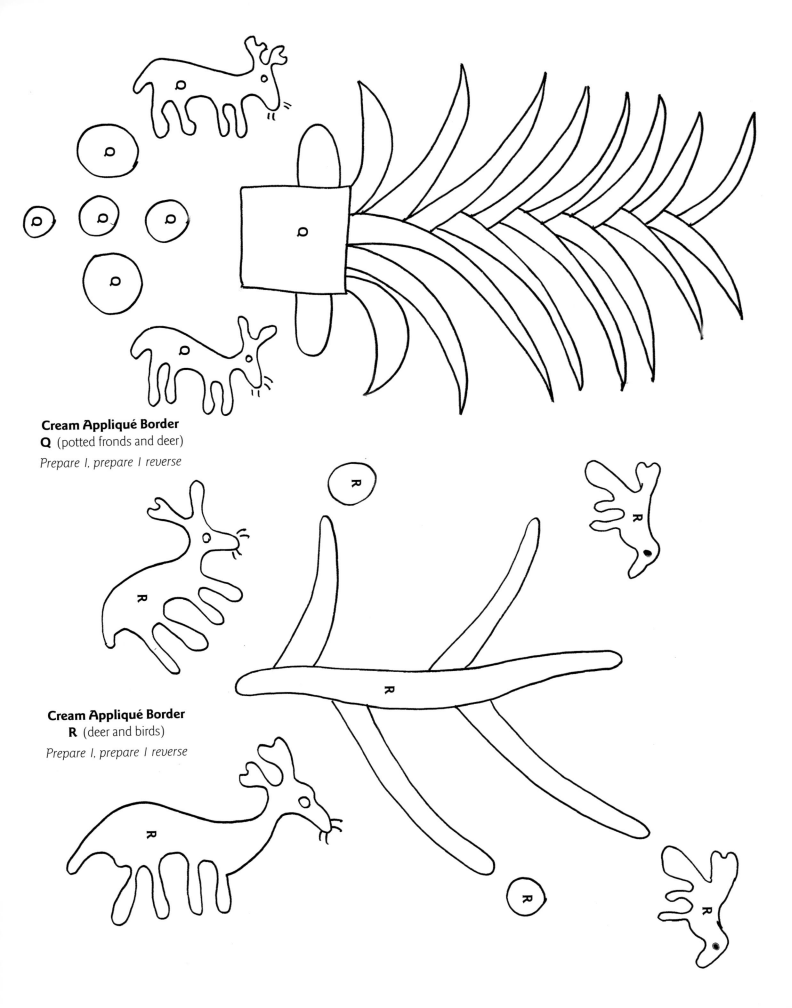

Cream Appliqué Border
Q (potted fronds and deer)

Prepare I, prepare I reverse

Cream Appliqué Border
R (deer and birds)

Prepare I, prepare I reverse

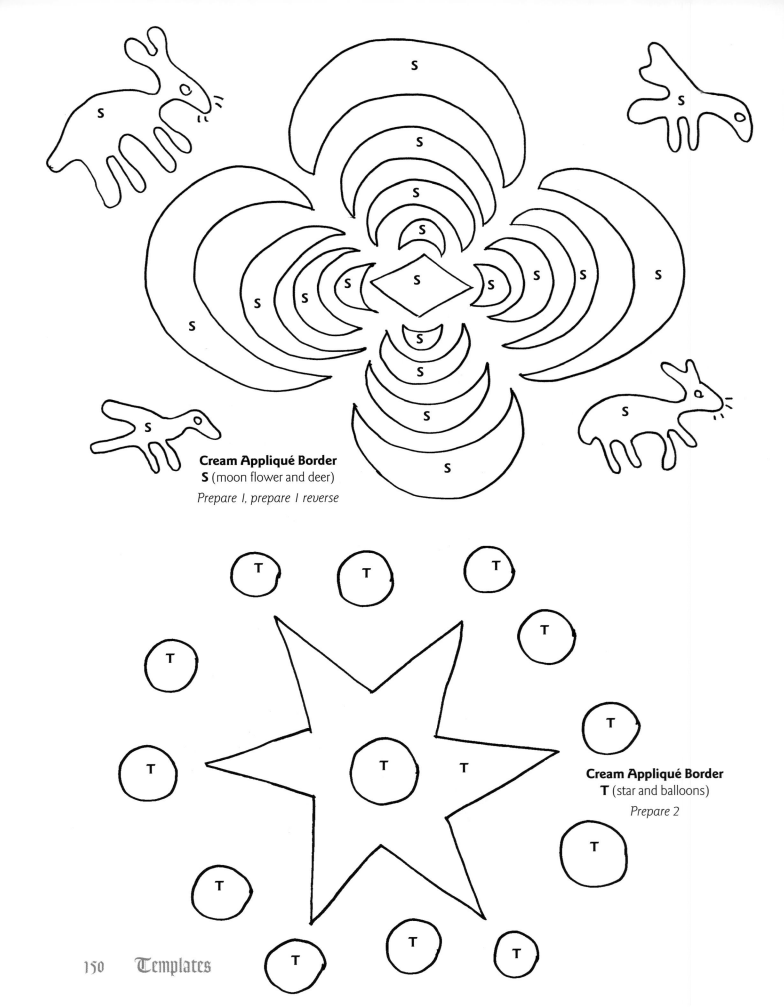

Cream Appliqué Border
S (moon flower and deer)
Prepare 1, prepare 1 reverse

Cream Appliqué Border
T (star and balloons)
Prepare 2

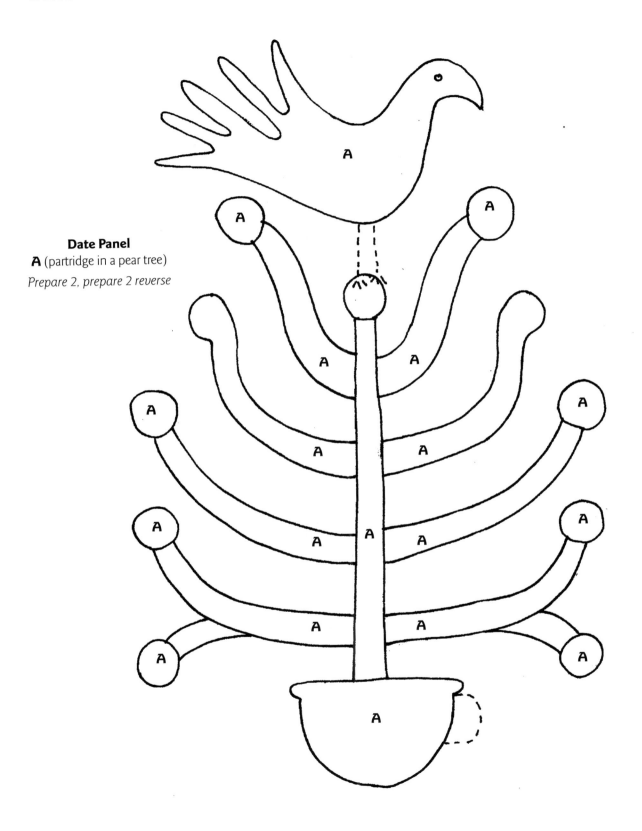

Date Panel
A (partridge in a pear tree)
Prepare 2, prepare 2 reverse

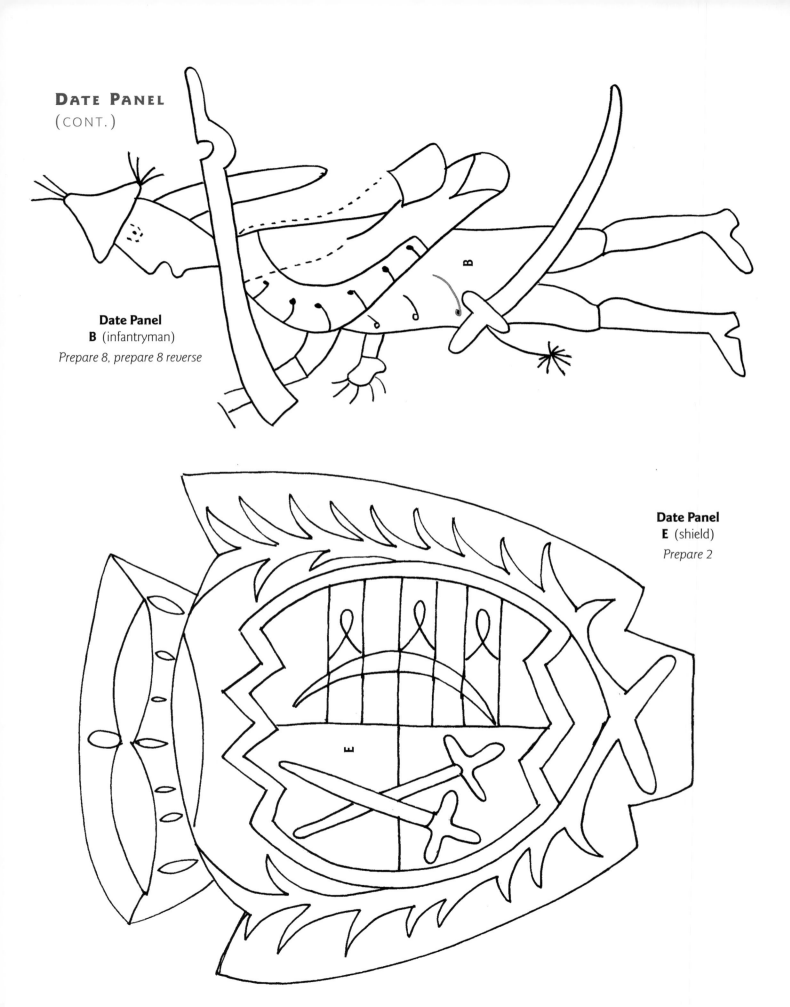

Date Panel
B (infantryman)
Prepare 8, prepare 8 reverse

B

Date Panel
E (shield)
Prepare 2

E

C

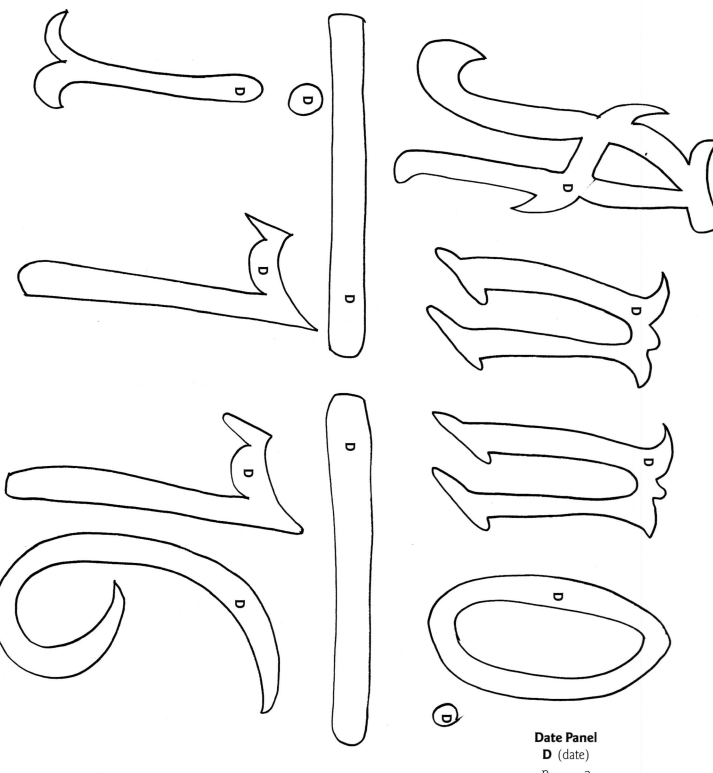

Date Panel
D (date)

Prepare 2
(turn "6" upside down for bottom panel)

1776 Sampler
B (small Bautzen block)
Prepare 1

Four Horsemen
D (short star point)
Prepare 8

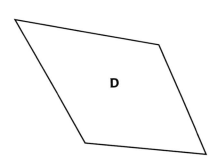

King of Eagles
C (bird wings)
Prepare 3

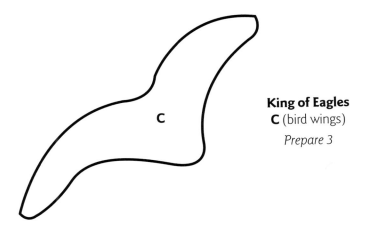

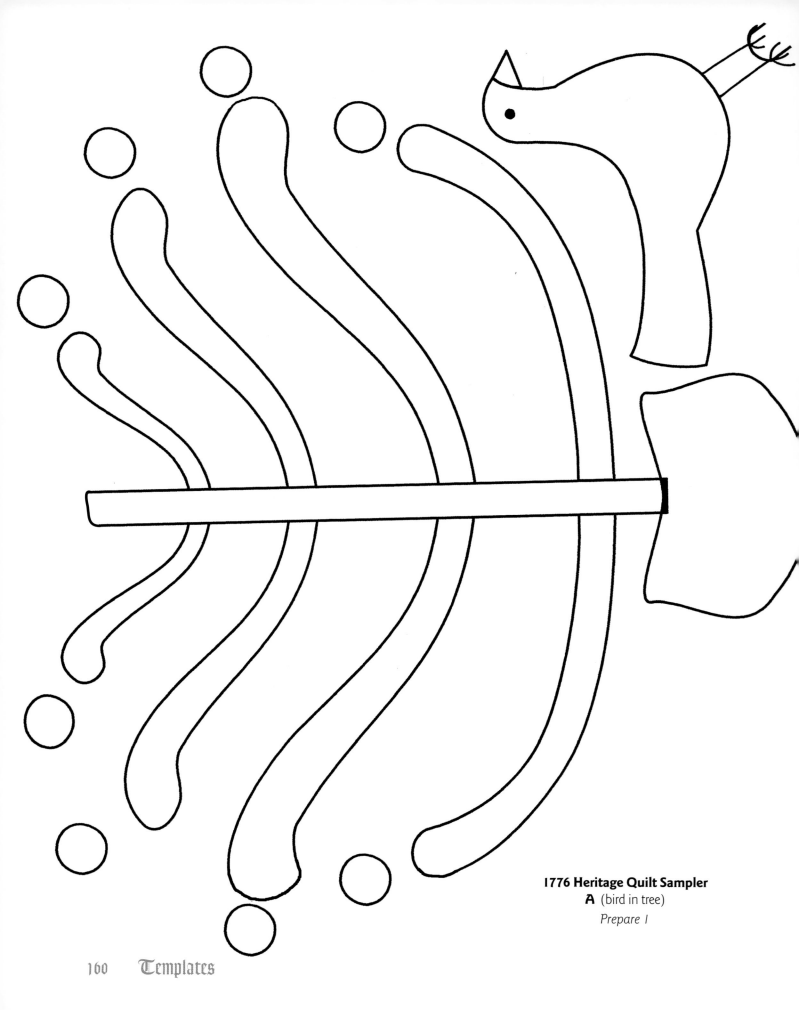

1776 Heritage Quilt Sampler
A (bird in tree)
Prepare 1

OFFSPRING QUILTS (CONT)

Appliqué Block Border
J (Wendish block)
Prepare 4

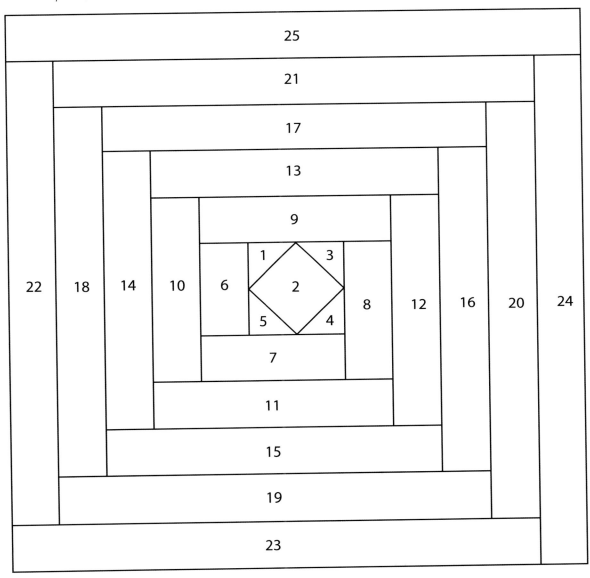

Acknowledgments & More

First and most important, I want to express my thanks to my husband Keith for his patience and support, and to our children—Suchada, Jamie, Rachael, Matthew, Joshua, Benjamin, Callie, and Jinda and their families—for their faith in me and my work. I grew up in an environment of artistic and musical expression inherited from a long line of noted artists. My father, Bedford Smedley, taught me the art of perfection and my mother, Shirley Smedley, with her many talents, taught me how to do many things. Mum creates amazing pieces of textile art, even now, in her late 70s.

My Aunt Laurel, who has the most wonderful imagination, challenged me to tell even better stories than she could create. I have always told stories—I thought it was what everyone did. I finally realized it wasn't quite like that, but it has taken me fifty years to write them down.

Joan Dougherty, my dearest friend, urges me to leap beyond the boundaries. We met by chance (or was it destiny?) eleven years ago. Not only was Joan with me when I first saw the photo of *1776*, she has encouraged me throughout my entire career in quilting.

Marti Michell suggested I share *1776* with the world. Marti's influence in the world of quilting is legendary, and I value her judgment with absolute awe.

Janet Rae inspired me with her knowledge of inlay appliqué and the history of quilting. She opened the doors to a different way of thinking about our historical inheritance.

Jackie Robinson was instrumental in helping me gain teaching acceptance in the USA. I met Jackie when she visited South Australia many years ago. After attending her classes, I maintain that she is one of the best quilting teachers I have ever known.

Cynthia McLeod has been my business partner for many years and a faithful companion on my journey into design and quilting. We began in a naïve fashion and developed a business to challenge the top designers in Australia, all from a shed in the back yard.

Jeanette Coombes is my friend, manager, and mentor. Together for thirty years, its amazing how our lives have blended over time.

The S & B (Stitch & Bitch) girls have been together for thirteen years. We meet weekly and have grown creatively and emotionally together, sharing wonderful and sad times.

My heartfelt thanks to the talented Retreating Angels for making the samples for the book and giving me so much support: Jan Munzberg, Jenny Loveder, Jane Green, Mary Heard, Pip Scholten, Liz Needle, Dianne Assheton, Chris O'Brien, Elvie Richardson, Vera Lloyd, Heather Bolt, Maureen Harper, Claire Warby, and Jeanette Coombes.

The Quilter's Cupboard in Hahndorf South Australia closed many years ago, but the proprietors are still in the quilting world. They unknowingly gave me a passion for quilting.

Lessa Siegele was one of my first teachers. Cynthia and I attended Lessa's weekly class for many years. We sat our machines on rickety card tables and nervously attempted to follow what everyone else was sewing. The older members guided us with patience.

I am grateful to Kaye England for having faith in me and to Mary Elizabeth Johnson for her guidance and encouragement.

Finally, where would I be without the kindness of that lovely janitor at the Bautzen Museum who acted as my host, let me into the building, and allowed me to photograph and view the original 1776 quilt? My debt to him is beyond payment.

BIBLIOGRAPHY

Baird, Ljiljana. *Quilts*: London, MQ Publications Ltd, 1994.

The Columbia Electronic Encyclopedia, Sixth Edition: New York; Columbia University Press; 2005. "Bavarian Succession, War of the" (Online at Columbia Encyclopedia).

Rae, Janet. *The Quilts of the British Isles*: New York; E.P. Dutton; 1987. Reprinted in 1996 by Deirdre McDonald Books, London.

von Gwinner, Schnuppe. *The History of the Patchwork Quilt Origins, Traditions and Symbols of a Textile Art*: West Chester, PA; Schiffer Publishing Ltd. 1988.

RESOURCES

Cherrywood Fabrics
P.O. Box 486
Brainerd, MN 56401
Tel: 888-298-0967
www.cherrywoodfabrics.com

Warm and Natural® Quilt Batting
The Warm™ Company
954 E. Union Street
Seattle, Washington 98122
Tel: 800-234-WARM
www.warmcompany.com

Metafil needles @
Sullivans USA, Inc.
4341 Middaugh Ave.
Downers Grove, IL 60515
Tel: 800-862-8586
Fax: 630-435-1532
www.sullivans.net

Wonder Under® fusible web
Pellon® Consumer Products
4720A Stone Drive
Tucker, Georgia 30084
Tel: 770-491-8001
www.pellonideas.com

Superior Threads
Post Office Box 1672
St. George, Utah 84771
Tel: 800-499-1777 or
435-652-1867
Fax: 435-628-6385
www.superiorthreads.com

Quilt Light® fabric stabilizer
Mountain Mist
2551 Crescentville Road
Cincinnati, Ohio 45241
Tel: 800-345-7150
Fax: 513-326-3911
www.mountainmist@leggett.com

The Applique Pressing Sheet™
Bear Thread Designs, Inc.
P.O. Box 1452
Highlands, Texas 77562
Tel: 281-462-0661
www.BearThreadDesigns.com

Index